CENTRE FOR EDUCATIONAL RESEARCH AND INNOVATION

EDUCATION POLICY ANALYSIS

2001

ORGANISATION FOR ECONOMIC CO-OPERATION AND DEVELOPMENT

ORGANISATION FOR ECONOMIC CO-OPERATION AND DEVELOPMENT

Pursuant to Article 1 of the Convention signed in Paris on 14th December 1960, and which came into force on 30th September 1961, the Organisation for Economic Co-operation and Development (OECD) shall promote policies designed:

- to achieve the highest sustainable economic growth and employment and a rising standard of living in Member countries, while maintaining financial stability, and thus to contribute to the development of the world economy;

- to contribute to sound economic expansion in Member as well as non-member countries in the process of economic development; and

- to contribute to the expansion of world trade on a multilateral, non-discriminatory basis in accordance with international obligations.

The original Member countries of the OECD are Austria, Belgium, Canada, Denmark, France, Germany, Greece, Iceland, Ireland, Italy, Luxembourg, the Netherlands, Norway, Portugal, Spain, Sweden, Switzerland, Turkey, the United Kingdom and the United States. The following countries became Members subsequently through accession at the dates indicated hereafter: Japan (28th April 1964), Finland (28th January 1969), Australia (7th June 1971), New Zealand (29th May 1973), Mexico (18th May 1994), the Czech Republic (21st December 1995), Hungary (7th May 1996), Poland (22nd November 1996), Korea (12th December 1996) and Slovak Republic (14th December 2000). The Commission of the European Communities takes part in the work of the OECD (Article 13 of the OECD Convention).

The Centre for Educational Research and Innovation was created in June 1968 by the Council of the Organisation for Economic Co-operation and Development and all Member countries of the OECD are participants.

The main objectives of the Centre are as follows:

- *analyse and develop research, innovation and key indicators in current and emerging education and learning issues, and their links to other sectors of policy;*

- *explore forward-looking coherent approaches to education and learning in the context of national and international cultural, social and economic change; and*

- *facilitate practical co-operation among Member countries and, where relevant, with non-member countries, in order to seek solutions and exchange views of educational problems of common interest.*

The Centre functions within the Organisation for Economic Co-operation and Development in accordance with the decisions of the Council of the Organisation, under the authority of the Secretary-General. It is supervised by a Governing Board composed of one national expert in its field of competence from each of the countries participating in its programme of work.

Publié en français sous le titre :
ANALYSE DES POLITIQUES D'ÉDUCATION - ÉDITION 2001

TABLE OF CONTENTS

INTRODUCTION 7

Chapter 1
LIFELONG LEARNING FOR ALL: POLICY DIRECTIONS

Summary 9

1. Introduction 10

2. The policy significance of lifelong learning 10
   2.1 Distinguishing features of the lifelong learning approach 10

3. Country approaches 12

4. Policy directions 17

5. Visibility and recognition of learning 18
   5.1 Informal learning and qualification 19
   5.2 Creating pathways 20
   5.3 Information and guidance 21

6. Foundations for lifelong learning 22
   6.1 Strengthening the motivation to learn for the young 22
   6.2 Motivating adult learners 24

7. Access and equity 26
   7.1 Gaps in access 26
   7.2 Diversity and access 28

8. Resources for lifelong learning 30
   8.1 Adequacy and allocation of resources 30
   8.2 Making more efficient use of resources 31
   8.3 Mobilising new resources 35

9. Policy co-ordination 36

10. Conclusions 39

References 41

Chapter 2
LIFELONG LEARNING FOR ALL: TAKING STOCK

Summary 43

1. Introduction 44

2. Taking stock of where countries stand: a systemic approach 44

3. Strengthening foundation and further learning 45
   3.1 Early childhood education and care (ECEC) 45
   3.2 Upper secondary education and training 47
   3.3 Tertiary education 50
   3.4 Continuing education and training 52

4. Increasing the affordability of lifelong learning 57
   4.1 Strengthening incentives to invest in lifelong learning 58
   4.2 Allocating more resources for lifelong learning 61
   4.3 Reducing the cost of capital for private sector investment in
       lifelong learning 63

5. Attempting a systemic assessment of lifelong learning 65

6. Conclusions 67

References 70

Chapter 3

CLOSING THE GAP: SECURING BENEFITS FOR ALL FROM EDUCATION AND TRAINING

Summary 73

1. Introduction 74

2. New and old reasons to care about educational equity 74

3. How widely has progress in educational attainment
   been shared among different groups? 76

    3.1 Equity and socio-economic background 76

    3.2 Equity and gender 79

    3.3 Equity and minority groups 82

    3.4 Equity and people with disabilities 83

4. The digital learning divide 84

    4.1 Do the digital divides increase existing inequalities? 86

    4.2 Access to ICTs in schools and in the labour market 88

5. Equity and lifelong learning 89

6. Conclusions 92

References 95

Chapter 4

COMPETENCIES FOR THE KNOWLEDGE ECONOMY

Summary 99

1. Introduction 100

2. The knowledge revolution 100

    2.1 Technological change and ICTs 100

    2.2 Upskilling of the labour force 102

3. What competencies are distinctive in the knowledge economy? 104

    3.1 Knowledge workers are highly education and/or highly literate 106

    3.2 Working competencies 109

4. Conclusions 112

Technical Annex 114

References 116

Chapter 5

WHAT FUTURE FOR OUR SCHOOLS?

Summary 119

1. Introduction 120

2. The OECD schooling scenarios 120

    2.1 The "status quo extrapolated" 122

    2.2 The "re-schooling" scenarios 127

    2.3 The "de-schooling" scenarios 133

3. Conclusions 138

References 141

STATISTICAL ANNEX: Data for the figures 143

List of Boxes, Figures and Tables

BOXES

1.1 Recognising informal learning 19
1.2 Making tertiary education "adult-friendly" 25
1.3 Danish taximeter system 33
1.4 Forestry project initiative in Sweden 34
1.5 Use of new technologies 35
3.1 Socio-economic background and access to tertiary education 77
3.2 Access of ethnic minorities to education 83
3.3 Equity and people with disabilities 84
4.1 Workplace competencies 106
4.2 Different definitions of knowledge workers 107

FIGURES

1.1 Participation in education and training over the life-span in OECD countries 18
2.1 Participation in pre-primary education for children aged 3, 1998 46
2.2 Progress towards achieving a minimum educational attainment level, 1998 48
2.3 Literacy scores and under-achievement rates of population aged 16-25 with upper secondary education, 1994-98 49
2.4 Progress towards increasing tertiary qualifications, 1998 51
2.5 Adult share in formal education by level, 1998 54
2.6 Adult participation in continuing education and training, 1994-98 56
2.7 Learning by older adults after formal education, 1994-98 57
2.8 Trends in expenditure per student and enrolment in tertiary education, 1990-96 59
2.9a Trends in public and private expenditure on all levels of education, 1990-96 60
2.9b Trends in public and private expenditure on tertiary education, 1990-96 61
3.1 College entrance by family income, United States, 1972-96 78
3.2 The relative earnings of women in successive generations 81
3.3 College entrance by racial or ethnic group, United States, 1972-96 82
3.4 Home and school access to computers in OECD countries, 1998 85
3.5 Percentage of U.S. households with Internet access by racial or ethnic group, 1998 and 2000 87
3.6 Home access to the Internet by gross income decile group in the UK, 1998-1999 and 1999-2000 87
3.7 Participation in job-related education and training by employed adults with different educational levels, 1994-95 91
4.1 Increasing importance of knowledge-based industries, 1985 and 1997 101
4.2 Growth in the proportion of the population and employment with tertiary-level qualifications, 1989-96 102
4.3 Upskilling in total employment growth, 1980-98 103
4.4 Skill requirements of knowledge workers in five domains, Canada 110

TABLES

1.1 Country approaches to lifelong learning 12
3.1 Student use of computer in 1st-8th grades in the United States, 1993-97 88
3.2 Percentage of workers, 18 year-old and over, using computers on the job, 1993 and 1997 in the United States 89
4.1 Employers' hiring criteria in the United States, 1994 and 1997 105
4.2 Education and literacy skills of knowledge workers 108

INTRODUCTION

"Lifelong learning will be essential for everyone as we move into the 21st century and has to be made accessible to all." This conclusion by Ministers of Education meeting at the OECD in 1996 laid down a very ambitious goal for policy. As the world moves increasingly to knowledge-based economies and societies, the emphasis given to this goal is not only right, but it must be reinforced.

There is robust evidence that knowledge and skills ("human capital") are an important determinant of economic growth and social development. Education and training systems play a crucial role in fostering the development of the human capital needed.

At the same time, new and old skills demanded in the labour market must be complemented by skills that help foster the social networks, norms and values ("social capital") that are essential for well-functioning democracies, with active participation by citizens. They can provide the basic resources of leadership and strong social networks that contribute to better government. Schools and institutions of learning can help create values for social co-operation, and so nurture social capital along with families, local communities and firms.

Education and training systems also must play an important role in promoting equity. Even though overall education levels have improved steadily over the past few decades, educational opportunities continue to be unevenly distributed. And there are new risks. As jobs expand in high-skilled occupations, new skills-based inequalities may emerge. Unequal access to, and use of, ICT may be reinforcing existing inequities through a new "digital divide".

So, it is not surprising that education emerges everywhere as the major pre-occupation of citizens and of governments. It should be our priority of priorities.

Yet today's consensus about the importance of "lifelong learning for all" is matched by agreement that it is far from easy to achieve it in practice. The OECD's work on education over the past five years has centred on the twin tasks of defining the Education Ministers' goal more concretely and drawing lessons on how it can be best pursued by Member countries. The present volume summarises some of the main results of our work and identifies future challenges.

Lifelong learning implies above all a *systemic* view, building strong linkages between learning at different stages of life and in a wide range of settings and partnerships rather than just looking at various forms of education and training provision in isolation from each other. The departures from existing views of schooling and learning are substantial and sharp: the recognition of a wide range of learning modes and pathways that are not constrained by rigid notions of formal primary, secondary and tertiary education; foundation skills that are not just about mastery of a basic school curriculum, but include motivation and capacity for self-directed learning; a system of resource allocation that is rational, efficient and adequate; and, the best and the brightest attracted to teaching at all levels, both challenged and prepared to encourage and enable everyone – from the earliest years through the *troisième* age – to learn and succeed.

These features of a well-functioning system of lifelong learning do not lend themselves to easy measurement or comparisons across countries. We know very little about the learning that takes place in informal settings of home, community and the workplace. We are, as yet, unable to understand fully the linkages that allow students to move between different types of schooling and learning beyond schooling. We have yet to produce convincing evidence that they are acquiring the motivation and information needed to take up opportunities at different stages of life. A major unfinished task is the development of measures that permit a better understanding of educational outcomes that are truly relevant to knowledge economies and societies.

The OECD, through its continuing work to refine and extend its international indicators of education and training systems and its peer reviews, is working hard with Member countries and other international organisations to fill these gaps.

This year will see a landmark in the assessment of 15 year-olds in school in almost all OECD countries with the publication in the autumn 2001 of the first results of the Programme for International Student Assessment. This will, for the first time, give a profile of how well students nearing the end of secondary education are prepared for adult life. It will allow the outcomes of schooling systems to be looked at not just in terms of mastery of the school curriculum or passing of school tests, but in relation to the underlying mission of education to prepare children for the challenges ahead of them in real life.

So the move towards the goal of lifelong learning for all remains a task in progress. The experience of the past five years does give grounds for optimism: overall, countries have moved forward. They are devoting more resources to learning, and more people are participating in it at different points in their lives. As the OECD and others become cleverer in monitoring outcomes, it will soon be possible to see more clearly whether all this learning activity is producing more of the skills that are really needed for the knowledge economy and society. ∎

D. J. JOHNSTON,
SECRETARY-GENERAL OF THE OECD

chapter 1

LIFELONG LEARNING FOR ALL POLICY DIRECTIONS

SUMMARY

In 1996, OECD Education Ministers adopted "Lifelong learning for all" as a policy framework. However access to learning is not yet a reality for all. Few countries have clearly defined the features of an overall system of lifelong learning, or attempted to implement one. Five key systemic features are identified here.

First, all learning should be recognised, not just formal courses. Systems for transferring credit are improving but gaps remain, especially in recognising informal learning. Good systems for informing and guiding learners, especially adults, remain elusive.

Second, lifelong learning requires good foundation skills among both the young and adults: particularly those with poor initial education. Motivation must be at the centre. This requires fundamental changes in curriculum and pedagogy, emphasising willingness to learn as much as content mastery.

Third, equitable access to learning requires a lifecycle perspective. Under-served groups such as pre-school children and adults must be a priority. Equally important is the quality of opportunities – diverse learning methods, courses and settings to cater for multiple learning needs.

Fourth, countries must evaluate resources according to lifecycle needs and deploy them effectively. Additional public resources may be needed, and new incentives to attract private resources.

Finally, the scope of lifelong learning goes beyond a single ministry. Policy co-ordination must involve many partners.

1. INTRODUCTION

This chapter summarises how the OECD has followed up the principle of "lifelong learning for all", by clarifying its meaning and looking at what countries are doing to implement it.

It is five years since OECD Education Ministers adopted "lifelong learning for all" as a guiding framework for their education policy, and asked the Organisation to investigate how best to implement lifelong learning strategies. This chapter summarises the OECD's response to that mandate. It attempts to answer the following questions:

– What is meant by strategies for lifelong learning, and how do they differ from other strategies?

– What are the key policy directions for implementing them?

– What are some examples of policies countries have adopted in practice to implement these strategies?

Section 2 sets out the essential features of the OECD view of lifelong learning strategies, and how these differ from strategies that do not adopt a lifelong learning approach. Section 3 gives an overview of how the lifelong learning approaches are being interpreted and applied in countries. The main body of the chapter reviews five areas of key importance to a lifelong learning strategy and illustrates them with some examples from country experiences. The final section presents some concluding remarks.

2. THE POLICY SIGNIFICANCE OF LIFELONG LEARNING

Lifelong learning has come to mean not just adult education, but all learning from cradle to grave in different settings.

The concept of lifelong learning, or lifelong education, became current in the 1970s. In its early development the concept was equated with giving adults access to formal courses at educational institutions. In choosing the goal of "lifelong learning for all" in 1996, OECD Education Ministers signalled a major departure by adopting a more comprehensive view. This goal covers all purposeful learning activity, from the cradle to the grave, that aims to improve knowledge and competencies for all individuals who wish to participate in learning activities. International organisations such as UNESCO and the European Commission have also adopted the more comprehensive approach.

2.1 Distinguishing features of the lifelong learning approach

The approach has four key features:

The lifelong learning framework emphasises that learning occurs during the whole course of a person's life. Formal education contributes to learning as do the non-formal and informal settings of home, the workplace, the community and society at large.[1] The key features of the lifelong learning approach are:

---

1. The terms *formal, non-formal and informal* learning are difficult to define precisely. According to the International Standard Classification for Education (UNESCO, 1997) *formal education* refers to the system of schools, colleges, universities and other formal educational institutions that normally contribute full-time education for children and young people. N*on-formal* education comprises any organised and sustained educational activities that do not correspond to this definition of formal education. It can take place both within and outside educational institutions and cater to persons of all ages. I*nformal learning* consists of all intended learning activities that cannot be classified as formal or non-formal learning. They are characterised by a relatively low level of organisation and may take place at the individual level (for example, self-directed learning) or at the group level (for example at the workplace or within the family). In this chapter, the term informal learning has been used to cover *both* non-formal and informal learning.

– First, it offers *a systemic view of learning*. The lifelong learning framework examines the demand for, and the supply of, learning opportunities, as part of a connected system covering the whole lifecycle and comprising all forms of formal and informal learning.

– taking a systemic view,

– Second, *the centrality of the learner*. The learner, and initiatives to cater for the *diversity* of learner needs, form the core of lifelong learning strategies. This signals a shift from educational policies that focus on formal institutional arrangements for learning. It represents a shift of attention from the supply of learning to the demand side.

– treating the learner as central,

– Third, the approach emphasises *the motivation to learn*, and draws attention to self-paced and self-directed learning.

– emphasising the motivation to learn, and ...

– Fourth, it takes a balanced view of the multiple objectives of education policy. These objectives relate to economic, social or cultural outcomes; to personal development; to citizenship and so on. The lifelong approach recognises that at the individual level the priorities among these objectives may change over the course of an individual's lifetime, and that each objective has to be taken into consideration in policy development.

– recognising education's multiple objectives.

Among these key characteristics, the first is the one that most distinguishes lifelong learning from other approaches to education policy. No competing approach is truly *systemic*: all are sector-specific. This central difference has important policy implications. In a systemic strategy:

The systemic approach is the key, underlining:

– People at each stage of life need not only to be given specific opportunities to learn new things, but also to be equipped and motivated to undertake *further learning*, where necessary organised and directed by themselves. Curricula, pedagogical practices and the organisation of learning all need to be examined from this perspective.

motivation to keep learning,

– Each learning setting needs to be *linked* to others, to enable individuals to make transitions and progress through various learning stages. Provision therefore needs to be structured in a way that creates appropriate linkages and pathways.

– links between stages,

– *Resources* for education cannot be looked at only in the context of separate sectors of formal provision. The lifelong learning approach raises questions about whether the distribution of education and training resources is optimal in promoting an individual's engagement in learning over the lifetime, and addresses resources for informal as well as formal learning.

– resource allocation choices,

– *No single ministry* has a monopoly of interest in lifelong learning. The approach requires a high level of co-ordination for developing and implementing policy.

– and co-ordination...

Thus, the 1990s "cradle-to-grave" vision of lifelong learning is substantially broader than the notions of adult education or recurrent education that previously shaped the debate on education policy. The next section reviews briefly some of the strategic approaches that countries have taken to implement this vision.

...and thus encompasses learning at all ages.

*Countries have embraced
this broad approach,
although applications tend
to be sector-specific.*

3. COUNTRY APPROACHES

Is support for lifelong learning only at the level of political rhetoric or are countries doing something practical about it? In a first attempt to answer this question, Table 1.1 presents illustrative information on how 15 Member countries are attempting to define and operationalise lifelong learning.

Several patterns emerge from the table:

– Lifelong learning is increasingly conceptualised by countries in terms of the broader "cradle-to-grave" view.

– Countries have not articulated explicit targets for the lifelong learning system taken as a whole. In those cases where targets have been identified they relate to specific sectors of provision.

– Many countries are introducing reforms at the sector level that are framed within the context of lifelong learning requirements. Countries differ in the emphasis they place on different sectors or types of provision of lifelong learning. For example, some countries cite lifelong learning as a reason to strengthen teaching and learning at the school level while others put the main emphasis on improving post-secondary and adult training opportunities.

– While all countries recognise both the economic and social objectives of lifelong learning, some emphasise employability and competitiveness while others pay special attention to personal development and citizenship.

Table 1.1 **Country approaches to lifelong learning**

AUSTRALIA

Document
Learning for Life: Review of Higher Education Financing and Policy (DEETYA, 1998).

Context
While there is not yet a formal government policy on lifelong learning, this and other reviews and papers have created an active debate, revealing widespread support for the overall principle (Candy and Crebart, 1997).

Main elements
Suggests that in its various forms (structured and unstructured), lifelong learning can provide individuals of all ages and backgrounds with skills and knowledge, enhancing job chances and personal enrichment.

AUSTRIA

Documents
Country Report (1998);
Working and Coalition Agreements of Governing Parties (1990, 1994, 1996, 2000);
Österreich neu regieren. Regierungsprogramm 2000.

Context
Education is a key part of the programme of Austrian governments, for economic and cultural reasons. Social partners participate actively in defining educational policies.

Main elements

Lifelong learning is a focal point of education policy, covering co-ordination, certification, innovative projects and improved information particularly in adult education and training; expanded and improved forms of co-operation between public and private institutions; increased access for disadvantaged persons; permeability between the dual system and the other education and training tracks; re-employment rights to permit employed persons to participate in continuing education and training; improvements to apprenticeship training; increases in schools' autonomy.

CANADA

Documents

Education Indicators in Canada (1999);
Report on Public Expectations of Post-secondary Education in Canada (1999).

Context

Lifelong learning is directly linked to skill acquisition, employment, higher earnings, and a fuller life. Knowledge acquisition at all stages of life is seen as vital to maintaining competitiveness in a global knowledge-based economy.

Main elements

Lifelong learning refers to learning over the life course. Federal, provincial and territorial governments have launched an early childhood development initiative, which recognizes the importance of the early years of childhood in the development of the child. It is anticipated that such measures will provide a strong foundation for participation in lifelong learning. Governments in Canada offer a variety of supports to increase participation for continuous learners, these include: implementing mechanisms that give incentives to save and invest in learning opportunities, improving and enhancing foundation skills such as literacy for adults, supporting informed decision making for investing in skills acquisition, and strengthening the acquisition of international competencies through international academic mobility.

CZECH REPUBLIC

Document

Country Report (1998)

Context

Lifelong learning is seen as a comprehensive process of vital importance. Immediate concern has concentrated on initial education.

Main elements

The process can be divided into two fundamental phases, namely initial education of all young people in the framework of the formal education system, and all subsequent continuing education and learning. Its purpose includes both preparing the student for his/her future profession and the personal cultivation of individuals or the cultivation of community life. Continuing education includes both the education of the employed and of the unemployed, and retired persons. It takes place in formal settings, provided by the state and private institutions, as well as in churches and enterprises. It is financed by varied sources. In the short and medium term, the policy preoccupations of public officials and social partners have been with the formal sector for initial education.

DENMARK

Document

Country Report (1998).

Context

Lifelong learning is viewed as a mandate for ensuring adequate learning opportunities for adults.

Main elements

A measure adopted in 1995 mentions the importance of initial education providing a sound foundation for further learning; it stressed wider opportunities to be provided through rationalisation of services by formal education institutions in order to allow freer choice by adults among learning opportunities as well as co-operation with industry. In May 2000, the Danish Parliament adopted a series of measures to tie continuing training and further education programmes together into a single coherent and transparent adult education system. The reforms were designed to widen access to learning for adults at all levels and in particular for those with low levels of education. The reforms aim to ensure wider recognition for knowledge and skills gained through work and life experience.

FINLAND

Documents
Country Report (1998);
The Joy of Learning: a national strategy for lifelong learning (Ministry of Education, 1997).

Context
One of the few countries that has published a national statement outlining its vision of lifelong learning.

Main elements
The government's development plan for the period 1999-2004 defines the following goals: offer one year of pre-school education for all children before the comprehensive school; help more young people to apply for upper secondary general or vocational education and complete their studies; develop student's learning skills in all sectors of the education system; increase the provision of non-university higher education; expand opportunities for adults to study for a university degree; expand opportunities for adults to study for upper secondary and post-secondary vocational qualifications and to pursue other studies that improve their employability and capacity for further learning; develop methods for recognising non-formal and informal learning.

FRANCE

Documents
Framework Law on Education (1989);
Five-year Law (1993).

Context
Established education as a top national priority.

Main elements
Sets objective of educating 80% of the youth population to upper secondary completion within 10 years. Five-year Law of 1993 adds the right of the young to vocational education.

HUNGARY

Document
Country Report (1998).

Context
The priority has been the strengthening of formal education.

Main elements
Lifelong learning is embodied in the "Strategy for the long-term development of Hungarian public education". It concerns modernisation of public education, and improvements in content that equip students to upgrade their skills and knowledge. The term includes organised learning for adults, subsequent to the completion of formal education, mainly related to the workplace. Non-formal self-education is not included. In the immediate term, the government is focusing on vocational training for young persons, training for the unemployed, at-risk workers, and expanding education opportunities for socially disadvantaged persons and ethnic minorities.

IRELAND

Document
Learning for Life: White Paper on Adult Education (Department of Education and Science, 2000).

Context
This document marks the adoption of lifelong learning as the governing principle of educational policy. It reflects on the role of adult education and sets out the government's policies for the future development of the sector.

Main elements
Recommends that adult education should be underpinned by three core principles: the recognition of the importance of both the different levels of educational provision and the quality of the early school experience in taking advantage from adult education; equality of access; and the necessity of serving a diverse population. Proposes that the government's priorities should be to expand the flexibility and supply of core programmes and services for adults, and to concentrate fee relief on those most at risk.

Documents
Country Report (1998);
Labour Agreement (1996).

Context
Lifelong learning was introduced as a policy objective by the government in 1996, in consultation with the social partners.

Main elements
Recognises the central role of human resources in production; envisions lifelong learning as a fundamental incentive to ensure competitiveness, supported by a balanced social model based on citizens' rights. Aims: to redefine the whole formative and learning system and the roles of institutions and individuals; to implement a united national strategy administered by districts under national direction; to foster motivation to learn; to develop alternative tertiary institutions. The concept addresses concerns about the quality and relevance of initial education, the gulf between formal education and the economy, the relatively low education levels of adults and young persons, and the need for ensuring that the learning process is more individualised and flexible.

ITALY

Documents
The First to Fourth and Final Reports on Educational Reform (National Council on Educational Reform, 1985-1987);
Report on Lifelong Integrated Education (Central Council for Education, 1981);
Country Report (1998).

Context
Japan was one of the first countries to express a comprehensive view of lifelong learning.

Main elements
"Lifelong integrated learning" was introduced in the 1960s, as a means for reforming Japan's school-centred education system, and improving re-training opportunities for adult workers. The concept implies that the education system promotes learning by individuals according to their own self-identified needs through life. Lifelong learning aims to remedy problems arising from the pressures of a "diploma society", relating learning less to school achievement and providing spiritual enrichment and better use of leisure time. It places the learner at the centre. It is also seen as a tool for regional development.

JAPAN

Documents
Country Report;
Education Reform for New Education System (Presidential Commission on Educational Reform, 1996).

Context
Recognised the need for a national framework of policies and infrastructure.

Main elements
While the concept of lifelong learning has long been valued philosophically in Korea, in practice it has been viewed as a luxury. The economic crisis of the late 1990s has pushed the government to pursue a more instrumental approach to it. The recently enacted Lifelong Learning Act expands job-related education and training activities for employed workers and the unemployed. At the same time, education reforms are being pursued to diversify student choice in schools, and increase learning opportunities that are accessible at any time, any place, and through varied media. Learning opportunities should in particular promote access, support services, and arrangements for credit transfer that open up study to people at times and places that meet their needs.

KOREA

Documents
Lifelong Learning: the Dutch Initiative (Ministry of Education, Culture and Science, 1998);
Country Report (1998).

Context
Elements of lifelong learning have been long established in the Netherlands. An action programme to implement specific lifelong learning policies was presented in 1998.

Main elements
By the 1980s, there were part-time alternatives for regular secondary and tertiary education, a diversified field of liberal adult education often run by the voluntary sector, a well-organised private sector, especially in the field of correspondence education and the relatively uncharted sector of on-the-job training. By the early 1990s, adult basic education for people with little or

NETHERLANDS

no schooling, and the Open University had been added. There also was rapid growth in training for the unemployed during the late 1980s and early 1990s. In the 1990s, there have been efforts to more closely link vocational training and business, to better translate labour market needs into school goals and curricula, to facilitate entry of non-public providers to learning markets, and to increase transparency of qualification requirements and learning outside the formal education sector. The 1998 action programme focuses on employability of employees and job seekers; employability of teaching staff; and prevention of disadvantages and reorientation of the education system towards lifelong learning.

NORWAY

Documents
Country Report;
The Competence Reform in Norway, Plan of Action 2000-2003 (Ministry of Education, Research and Church Affairs, 2000).

Context
Norway started the process of implementing a competence reform for adults in 1999. The reform creates the basis for a national plan of action for continuing education and training and adult education.

Main elements
The reforms are being implemented according to a broad "cradle-to-grave" view of lifelong learning. The concept has expanded to embrace the complete life-span including basic education for children and young people. The reforms seek to help meet the need for competence in society, in the workplace and at the level of the individual. Priorities include: a good basic education (Reform '94); primary and lower secondary education (Reform '97); adaptation of educational programmes more to the needs of adults; organisation of framework conditions so as to ensure competence building for the individual; encouragement of participation and competence building in businesses; documentation and evaluation of non-formal learning; creation of conditions preventing exclusion; provision of information about educational options.

SWEDEN

Documents
Country Report (1998);
Lifelong Learning and Lifewide Learning (National Agency for Education, 2000).

Context
The National Agency for Education has a special action programme for lifelong learning. The action programme is intended to create an overview of the anatomy of lifelong learning in Sweden and to identify and analyse key issues in a strategy for lifelong learning.

Main elements
Recognises that lifelong learning is an attitude to learning. The great challenge is to create amongst all citizens a desire to learn and the opportunities for realising this. The lifelong learning framework used has two dimensions: the individual learns throughout a life-span; and formal, non-formal and informal learning are equally important. Identifies three principal sectors in which lifelong learning develops: the educational system; the labour market; and civil society. Recognises that lifelong learning requires adequate co-ordination between policy areas. Indicates the need for a shift in responsibility from the public to the private and civil spheres. Stresses the importance of "putting the individual in the centre". Limits state responsibility to the creation of conditions and incentives for individuals and other actors to invest in education and learning.

UNITED KINGDOM

Document
The Learning Age: a Renaissance for a New Britain (Department for Education and Employment, 1998).

Context
Green Paper for England setting out the broad strategy of the new Labour government, seeking consultation on a range of issues.

Main elements
Advocates a regard for learning at all ages, from basic literacy to advanced scholarship, including formal and informal learning. Learning is seen as the key to prosperity and the foundation of success. The development of the spiritual side of individuals and of citizenship

are considered important alongside economic objectives; the green paper stresses preparing citizens for active participation in all spheres. Government role is seen as enabling citizens to take responsibility for themselves. Proposals include expanding further and higher education, creating the "University for Industry", setting up individual learning accounts and promoting post-16 education, adult literacy, higher skill levels, and better teaching and learning standards.

Source: The information in the table draws upon national reports prepared by countries which participated in OECD's activity on financing lifelong learning. This information has been supplemented by other national statements that have become available recently.

4. POLICY DIRECTIONS

Despite the popularity of the lifelong learning concept, Figure 1.1 shows that in terms of participation in organised learning activity, "lifelong learning for all" is far from being a reality in OECD countries.[2] What can countries do to implement strategies for "lifelong learning for all"? What are the key areas of such a system where policy reforms should be directed as a priority? What are the desirable features of such policy reforms?

In setting priorities for making lifelong learning a reality...

In seeking to answer these questions, a review of the work done under the current OECD mandate suggests action in the following five areas of the life-long learning system:

... countries should consider action in five areas...

a) recognising all forms of learning, not just formal courses of study;

b) developing foundation skills that are wider than those traditionally identified as central, including in particular motivation and the capacity for self-directed learning;

c) reformulating access and equity priorities in a lifelong context – by looking at opportunities available to individuals across their life cycle and different learning settings;

d) considering resource allocation across all sectors and settings;

e) ensuring collaboration among a wide range of partners including ministries other than education.

These five areas are discussed below, and, in each case, the system-wide issue is discussed in terms of broad policy directions in the specific sectors of provision where the principles are applied in practice. These guidelines are illustrated with specific examples taken from country experiences.

... and are doing so in ways illustrated below.

2. Figure 1.1 brings together enrolment information in formal education and participation in adult education and training averaged (unweighted) for 18 OECD countries. The data combine two very different concepts and coverage, one based on full-time education and the other largely on part-time participation, defined as participation in any organised learning activity over a twelve-month period. The formal education data are drawn from national records of students enrolled in educational institutions and refer to 1998. The adult education and training data are based on a question in the International Adult Literacy Survey (IALS) about whether the respondent has participated in any organised learning activity for any length of time during the previous twelve months and refer to 1998 (or earlier in some countries). All full-time students aged 16-24 are left out of this calculation to avoid double-counting for the overlapping age-groups.

> Enrolment in formal
> education is virtually
> universal during ages 4
> to 15, but participation in
> some form of organised
> learning activity is not a
> reality for all.

Figure 1.1 Participation in education and training over the life-span in OECD countries[1]

Percentage of age cohort enrolled in formal education (age 3 to 29) and participation in adult education and training (age 16 to 65), unweighted mean for 18 countries, 1998

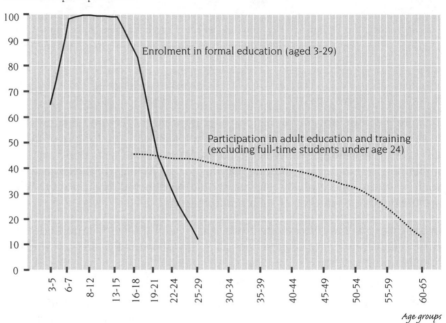

Enrolment and participation rates

Enrolment in formal education (aged 3-29)

Participation in adult education and training (excluding full-time students under age 24)

Age groups

1. Australia, Belgium, Canada, Czech Republic, Denmark, Finland, Germany, Hungary, Ireland, Netherlands, New Zealand, Norway, Poland, Portugal, Sweden, Switzerland, United Kingdom, United States.
Sources: OECD Education Database and International Adult Literacy Survey Database. ....
Data for Figure 1.1, p. 144.

However, the examples mostly relate to recent initiatives that have not been evaluated – they are best viewed as illustrations, not necessarily models of best practice.

5. VISIBILITY AND RECOGNITION OF LEARNING

> *Different forms of learning
> need to be recognised
> according to the true benefits
> they bring.*

Learning takes many forms and takes place in many different settings, from formal courses in schools or colleges to various types of experience in families, communities and workplaces. All types of learning need to be recognised and become visible, according to their content, quality and outcomes rather than their location and form, for three main reasons. First, better recognition will include more learning within qualification systems, and qualifications systems are important in giving access to further learning and to jobs. Second, better pathways are needed between different sectors of education to avoid educational dead-ends. Third, learners need better "signposts" to allow them to obtain the information and guidance needed to take full advantage of wider learning opportunities.

Box 1.1 **Recognising informal learning**

In **France**, 1985 legislation took steps to introduce a full-scale system for the identification and assessment of informal and experiential learning. It gave employees a right to an assessment (the *bilan de compétence*) of their professional and personal competencies as well as their motivation and aptitudes in order to facilitate both their professional and educational plans and careers (Colardyn, 1996). A national network of over 700 public and private organisations has been created that annually provides some 125 000 individual assessments. However, the *bilan de compétence* does not recognise competence in a way that leads to an educational qualification. To address this, 1992 legislation provided for the validation of skills acquired through work experience in a way that is directly linked to national qualifications.

Since the 1950s, **Norway** has had a legal basis for adult candidates to take final apprenticeship examinations based on their practical work experience. In principle, candidates must take the same final examination as apprentices. However, in practice they are exempted from general subjects, such as the Norwegian language and social studies. Use of this "Section 20" provision remained moderate during the 1970s and 1980s, but expanded greatly in the 1990s. By 1995, 41% of all trade certificates were awarded to Section 20 candidates. More recently, Norway has explored wider mechanisms for recognising informal learning. In 1999, it began establishing a national system to document and recognise, in the workplace and in education, adults' informal learning. Pilot projects have begun to relate informal learning both to upper secondary education and to higher education using a mix of written and oral tests, age, self-evaluation, and relevant work experience. A May 2000 bill proposed allowing universities and colleges to admit students without formal entrance qualifications on the basis of age (25 years or more) and informal learning, and also giving them credit in their studies for non-formal learning. A range of projects has been initiated to investigate how informal learning acquired in family and community settings, and through work experience, can be identified, assessed and recognised in order to provide access to occupations, to provide credit or exemptions within formal education, and to provide certification.

5.1 Informal learning and qualification

Giving due recognition to learning that occurs outside formal education is complex and difficult. It requires standards and learning outcomes to be defined, against which such learning can be assessed. It requires agreed assessment techniques to be developed and agreement on recognition methods and portability of credits. Addressing these issues requires the active commitment and engagement of a number of stakeholders, within and between different education sectors as well as between those in education and groups such as employers and trade unions. And it requires policy makers to move beyond the development of attractive conceptual models to the creation of practical tools that are affordable and that can easily be implemented.

Systems to give due credit to non-formal learning must be carefully worked out through partnerships…

During the 1990s, many OECD countries struggled to give greater visibility to informal learning: to assess and recognise it; to give credit towards qualifications; and to provide forms of recognition that can enhance careers. However,

…but progress in doing so can be slow.

in many countries, giving greater visibility to informal learning has proven to be difficult. Countries such as Germany and Austria have been reluctant to embrace the concept, perhaps in part due to the success of their strong apprenticeship systems. In the Southern European countries, the notion has been greeted positively, but legal and political moves to introduce the principle have often not been matched by substantial reform in practice. In the United Kingdom, acceptance of such recognition has been enthusiastic (Bjørnåvold, 2000). However, the actual realisation of a workable system has proven difficult: issues such as the development of acceptable qualifications standards, and the reliability, validity and costs of assessments loom large (Wolf, 1995).

Notwithstanding these real barriers to recognition and validation of non-formal learning, models do exist that countries can learn from. Box 1.1 above describes interesting experiences in this vein, from France and Norway.

5.2 Creating pathways

Many countries are reforming learning pathways to make progression easier...

During the 1990s, many OECD countries have been attempting to lay a better foundation for learning beyond the compulsory and upper secondary stages, and to eliminate educational dead-ends. This has involved tackling key barriers, by strengthening links between:

– General and vocational education at upper-secondary level, by bringing them closer together;

– Upper-secondary vocational education and tertiary study, by making it easier to progress from the former to the latter;

– Non-university and university-level tertiary education, by making it easier to move between them (OECD, 1998a; OECD, 2000a).

... for example by opening up new options to vocational students...

Hungary, Norway and Sweden increased the general education content of upper-secondary vocational pathways. The aim was to give students wider general and conceptual knowledge and skills that they would need in working life. At the same time people following these pathways were given better access to tertiary study. Denmark introduced reforms to achieve the same objectives. Norwegian evidence shows that these initiatives have made vocational pathways more attractive. In Sweden, students from nearly all vocational areas are now following through to further studies. However, in both cases some difficulties have arisen. Weaker students can struggle to cope with the higher demands of the general education subjects. Teachers sometimes find it difficult to relate the increased general education content clearly to the world of work. And vocational students normally gain access to further study only if they have done well in general subjects – with an implicit under-valuing of vocational studies themselves.

... including some courses qualifying students for both further study and work...

One mechanism that Austria has adopted to create pathways from upper secondary vocational education to tertiary education is "double qualifying" programmes, that qualify students both for work and for tertiary entry. These programmes are very demanding, and involve extending the total duration of upper secondary study. This initiative and Switzerland's *maturité professionelle*, which has a similar outcome, have proven to be highly popular, both with young people and with employers. At the same time they can carry the risk of marginalising and reducing the status of the remaining vocational pathways that do not lead to tertiary study.

OECD countries have also improved pathways from secondary to tertiary education in other ways. One is to offer tertiary-level studies in secondary schools as in New Zealand and Advanced Placement programmes in the United States. Belgium (Flemish Community), France and the Netherlands have launched initiatives to encourage and enable students to consider the range of tertiary study options and their requirements. The Dutch "study house" initiative attempts to acquaint students early with the teaching and learning methods found at tertiary level. In New Zealand, the Qualifications Framework is an important aspect of an infrastructure that allows a learner to build a qualification. Experiments with the development of more unified approaches to national qualification systems – for example in the United Kingdom, Mexico and New Zealand – can be seen as attempts to grapple with many of the same issues.

... or by introducing elements of tertiary study into secondary education...

The difficulties that have been experienced in creating links between upper secondary general and vocational education, and between upper secondary education and tertiary study, particularly at university level, are matched by barriers encountered in creating learning pathways between non-university-level tertiary study and university-level tertiary study. Credit transfer arrangements between sectors of tertiary education have not been easy to negotiate, and their translation into actual student flows has generally proven problematic. Recognition of prior learning, whether across tertiary education sectors or institutions or from outside the formal tertiary education system, remains an important target for tertiary education policy. Highly flexible non-university-level tertiary institutions – such as the Community Colleges in North America and Australia's technical and further education (TAFE) Colleges – can have many advantages in creating learning pathways. They can provide flexible entry points, offer remedial and foundation programmes for those lacking entry prerequisites, and provide programmes at several levels to allow individual students to meet a range of learning needs within a single institution.

... or improving transfer between different kinds of tertiary institution. But building such links has proven problematic.

5.3 Information and guidance

Flexible learning pathways make appropriate "signposts" for lifelong learners essential. Only sophisticated and effective education and employment information and guidance systems will allow students to find their way along the paths. Traditionally such services have received a low priority in many OECD countries. Inconsistencies within countries in objectives, resourcing, staff qualifications and delivery methods are striking. And whatever the weaknesses of national information and guidance services for youth, weaknesses and gaps in services for adults are even more evident.

The guidance and information needed has been lacking...

Such services traditionally have been delivered in one of two main ways: on a one-to-one basis by professional counsellors; or by specialist careers teachers

... and traditional delivery mechanisms are inadequate...

within classrooms. The first model is very expensive when translated into greatly increased access. The second is generally not suitable to deliver careers services to adults. The challenge is to build comprehensive information and educational and occupational guidance systems, catering for both adults and youth, that are both high-quality and affordable.

... but the UK has illustrated a way of informing adults of what is available.

The United Kingdom's *Learndirect* service is an innovative approach. Launched in 1998, it provides a single, free-access telephone number that allows adults[3] to obtain national information about learning opportunities. Initial inquiries are handled by basic information providers, with careers advisers available on-line for those with more complex inquiries: referral to the Careers Service is available for those whose needs cannot be met on the telephone. *Learndirect's* telephone help-line is complemented by web-based access. Its site also provides users with access to basic self-assessment techniques that can narrow information searches according to personal interests and skills.

6. FOUNDATIONS FOR LIFELONG LEARNING

Learning foundations require more than just access to basic schooling.

Solid foundations for learning need to be established across the lifespan, not just by giving universal access to primary education. A broader conception requires countries to improve access to early childhood education, to improve young people's motivation to learn and their capacity to learn independently, and to address learning deficiencies in adults, as well as to focus on achievement standards and to try to raise the level of competence for all. Issues of access to early childhood education are discussed below in Section 7.1. This section discusses approaches to raising the motivation to learn among young people and adults.

6.1 Strengthening the motivation to learn for the young

Young people need to be better motivated within school...

Motivation to learn can be strengthened in several ways within the formal education system: by providing wider opportunities for work-based learning in upper secondary schools, by enhancing opportunities for student choice, by encouraging co-operation with institutions outside the school, by introducing more learner-centred pedagogy, and by introducing anti-bullying strategies to enhance student enjoyment of school and self-esteem.

... and encouraged to complete upper-secondary education...

To reinforce a solid basis for later learning during the transition phase, policies need to encourage both high rates of upper secondary completion and qualification and the attainment of strong basic skills by the end of secondary education. Evidence shows that young people without an upper secondary qualification and without strong literacy skills are among the least likely to participate in further education and training as adults, or as adults to take part in training within enterprises (OECD and Statistics Canada, 2000). Across OECD countries, some one in four 20-24 year-olds have not completed upper secondary education (see Chapter 2). However, there is wide variation across countries: from one in ten or less in countries such as Korea, the Czech Republic and Norway to a third or more in Italy, Spain, Turkey and Portugal.

---

3. Three quarters or more of all calls (around 1.7 million in 2000) to *Learndirect* are from those aged 25 or over.

An essential element of policies to encourage upper secondary school completion must be strategies to prevent students from leaving school early, and to identify and quickly re-enrol those who drop-out, allowing and encouraging them to complete a full upper secondary qualification. Denmark, Norway and Sweden are notable for the success with which they have put in place such strategies during the 1990s. They have been effective in keeping the number of early school leavers low, in reducing the proportion of school leavers who move immediately from school to unemployment,[4] and in substantially reducing the incidence of long-term unemployment among those under the age of 20.

... with intervention to address drop-out...

If policies during the transition phase are to strengthen students' motivation to learn, they need to provide a range of appropriate learning environments and make provision for a range of learning styles. In practical terms, this requires the provision of:

...and appropriate learning styles, which:

– **Active and project-based learning**, within both general and vocational education pathways, giving young people opportunities to see learning in a practical context outside school, to assume control over their own learning, to develop a sense of civic responsibility, and to build links between theory and practice. In the United States, substantial emphasis has been put upon community service-based learning during the 1990s to achieve these goals. In Norway, formal requirements now exist for all students to take part in project-based learning on a regular basis, and teacher training and staff development programmes have been adapted to provide teachers with the skills to manage this form of learning.

– make learning a more active and practical,

– **A wide range of vocational education programmes**, able to meet the developing occupational interests and career goals of the full range of students, and broader combinations of general and vocational education, allowing the latter to develop skills and knowledge as a foundation for further education and training. Countries in which the great majority of upper secondary students take part in general education programmes experience particular problems in retaining motivation unless, as in Japan, steps are taken to introduce a strong link between school performance and access to jobs.

– meet students' vocational needs,

– **Opportunities to combine classroom learning with learning in work settings**. This is important to allow an early connection to be established between learning and working life in order to motivate students as well as to increase employment prospects. Such combinations have been common for many years in countries with strong apprenticeship traditions such as Germany and Switzerland. During the 1990s, Norway has strengthened its apprenticeship system to encourage higher participation by young people, including through the restructuring of training wages and of financial incentives for employers. In some countries where apprenticeship traditions have not always been strong – such as Australia, Canada, Sweden and the United States – notable effort has been devoted during the 1990s to the creation of school-managed

– give students work place experience, insuring that learning is well-managed and of high quality.

4. This is a particularly important policy outcome, given the strong relationship that exists between moving directly from school to unemployment and longer-term difficulties in settling into a stable employment pattern (OECD, 1998c).

workplace experience programmes. Whilst the evidence on the impact of these programmes on later employment remains unclear, there seems little doubt that they are highly popular with, and motivating for, young people. If opportunities are to be created for young people to learn in real work settings, appropriate incentives both for them and for employers need to be put in place. In the case of apprenticeship, these incentives typically take the form of youth training wages. Setting the latter at levels that provide appropriate incentives to both parties, and encourage wide participation, is a matter that goes beyond Education Ministries, involving the social partners and Labour Ministries. The incentives that are required to encourage school-managed workplace experience programmes to expand are less clear. OECD evidence suggests that the quality of the programmes is important in creating incentives for both parties. This in turn depends upon the quality of the support provided by education systems and the roles that employers are encouraged to play in programme design and management.

6.2 Motivating adult learners

Adults too need to be motivated...

Recent research has highlighted some of the techniques that are successful in motivating adult learners (U.S. Department of Education and OECD, 1999; OECD, 1999*g*). In general, adults are most motivated when they draw on past experience, when learning is located in the context of their own lives, when it is applied to real problems and when they have choice and control over what they learn. Preliminary results from the ongoing Thematic Review of Adult Learning suggest some more specific policy lessons:

– by teaching them in distinctive ways,

– **The need for appropriate teaching methods.** Recent research shows that where teaching does not suit the specific learning requirements of adults, they tend not to participate. Adults do not learn in the same way as children. Trainers and teachers of adults require specific training, to enable them to use techniques specific to adults in both formal and informal learning. Experience, for example in Sweden's Folk High Schools, shows that adult students prefer facilities that are not shared with young pupils. Developing settings for learning that are adult-centred, such as Sweden's Folk High Schools, Denmark's AMU and VUC Centres, or Australia's TAFE colleges, can help raise adult participation (see Box 1.2).

– by making learning more convenient for them,

– **The need for flexibility in the scheduling and practicalities of adult learning.** Adults typically need options allowing them to progress at an individually determined pace, schedules that take into account such factors as work hours and/or children's school hours, easy access to transport facilities, and the availability of day-care facilities for children. The use of ICTs can be of great assistance in offering greater flexibility. Distance learning is an available option that can provide learning to people who would not otherwise have the chance. However, while ICTs can be of great help, participation should not be limited to those who have access to it. A key to the success of the Open University in the United Kingdom has been its use of regular mail, for example.

– and by attracting those who have been put off learning,

– **The importance of targeting adults who are hard to reach.** One approach with positive results is to separate the learning experience from assessment of outcomes, in an attempt to make learning enjoyable. For some adults, better results are obtained if learning is approached as a fun activity, and not only connected to better wages, promotions or grades. A "soft entrance" into learning through introductory or orientation courses on how to learn, or short seminar courses without grades, can ease the entrance into the adult learning process. This approach is used by the Nordic Study Circles (in Sweden and Norway), the School-clubs Migros in Switzerland, and the EDAP programme in the United Kingdom.

A culture of learning is important for promoting adult learning. Such a culture has to be embedded in the whole society and not only confined to the educational system. An important determinant of this culture of learning is the degree to which governments and the social partners are convinced of the importance of the need to refresh and upgrade adult skills.

...but more generally by developing a learning culture

Box 1.2 Making tertiary education "adult-friendly"

Australia has a very large "adult-friendly" non-university-level tertiary education system. The largest element of the system is a network of 74 government-funded Technical and Further Education (TAFE) colleges at more than 100 campuses. These have much in common with the Community Colleges in Canada and the United States. The public system also includes some community-based providers, training providers in private organisations, enterprises and some provision within university-level tertiary institutions. Courses are provided in a very wide range of vocational fields, and at a wide variety of levels. Provision includes both programmes that lead to formal qualifications within a national qualifications framework and programmes that do not. Programmes can meet a wide range of educational purposes, ranging from the provision of complete recognised vocational qualifications; to the updating of specific vocational skills; to remedying deficiencies in basic education; to preparation for university level studies; to hobby and recreational courses.

Colleges are widely dispersed geographically, and offer instruction on a full-time, part-time and distance-education basis. Most students enrol on a part-time basis, with the annual hours of attendance per student averaging around 200. Colleges are commonly open on evenings and at times on weekends, as well as during the day. Courses are organised on a modular basis, and students are able to enrol for specific modules as well as for a complete course. Around two-thirds of students enrol in programmes that lead to a formal national qualification, and a third in programmes that do not. Entry requirements are flexible, and commonly recognise work experience as well as formal secondary education qualifications. Many courses, particularly those that do not lead to formal qualifications, do not specify upper secondary qualifications as an entry requirement. Assessment procedures are also flexible, with around 6% of all assessments being made on the basis of prior learning or through credit granted for subjects completed elsewhere.

This has resulted in a system that is very "user-friendly" for adults, and in which adult participation has grown substantially during the 1990s. At the end of the 1990s, some one in eight Australians of working age (15-64) were participating in the system: among those aged over 30 around one in fourteen were participating. Between 1990 and 1999, total student numbers grew by 70%. However, the number of students aged 25 and over grew by 105% and the number aged 30 and over increased by 119%. In 1999 students aged 25 and over accounted for nearly two thirds of all students, and those aged 30 and over for almost half.

*Equity can be seen in terms
both of gaps in provision
and of serving diverse needs.*

7. ACCESS AND EQUITY

Access and equity are enduring concerns in education. Chapter 3 in this volume discusses equity issues in much greater detail and also addresses the emerging risk of a "digital divide". It highlights the "vicious circle" of some inequities that can only be broken through preventive action, which can be cost-effective in avoiding social expenditures in later phases of the life cycle. The focus here is the particular light that the lifelong learning framework throws on access and equity issues. These can be looked at in two ways. First, what provision is made, and how many people participate? Gaps in access are particularly evident in the areas of early childhood and adult years. Second, how do systems provide for increasingly diverse learner needs? As was noted in the preceding section, increased diversity of learning methods and options can help raise upper secondary completion rates and combat early school leaving. They can also be a major factor in raising access to tertiary education and adult learning.

7.1 Gaps in access

Early childhood education and care services

*In early childhood, countries
differ both in the level of
provision...*

In about half of the OECD countries with relevant data, fewer than half of children participate in pre-school programmes before age 4. OECD countries have been prompted in recent years to expand services for young children in order to raise women's participation in the labour market. But more fundamentally, high-quality, early learning environments form part of the foundation stage of lifelong learning. Neurological research suggests that brain development is remarkable in the early years. Research on the effects of programmes for young children suggests also that those who participate in a quality early childhood education and care environment are likely to develop higher-order reasoning and problem-solving skills.[5] They are also helped to make effective transitions to compulsory schooling, to be more co-operative and considerate of others, and to develop greater self-esteem. Thus early childhood education and care has the potential to maximise children's motivation and to prepare them for a lifetime of learning (OECD, 1999a).

*...and in their approach
and objectives...*

There are considerable differences among OECD countries in the importance they attach to education in the early years. There are also differences in how educational purposes might best be approached. In countries such as Denmark, Sweden, Finland, Norway and Italy, the educational emphasis tends to be placed upon the social and personal development of the child, with early childhood largely being seen as a phase in its own right. In the case of Denmark, this philosophy results in deliberate decisions to postpone the development of literacy and numeracy skills until the beginning of compulsory schooling. In other countries, such as the United States and the United Kingdom, the educational emphasis within early childhood services tends to be upon using these as a way to prepare the young child for primary schooling, and a stronger stress is placed upon the development of literacy and numeracy skills. These

---

5. Early childhood education and care includes all arrangements for children from birth to compulsory school age, regardless of setting, formality, funding, opening hours, or programme content. Within this framework, "care" and "education" are treated as inseparable concepts with regard to policies and provision for young children.

two approaches have much in common and are often pursued simultaneously, but they do highlight an important, and unresolved, debate about appropriate ways to use the early childhood services to lay a foundation for lifelong learning. Should the kindergarten encourage children to acquire rudimentary literacy and numeracy skills (fine motor skills, recognition of shapes, decoding and the like) or should it promote the child's social skills, aptitude for discovery learning, and pleasure in learning in the belief that these are equally as important for later learning? What degree of emphasis should be placed upon each of these strategies?

Despite these differences and the unresolved questions, the Thematic Review of Early Childhood Education and Care Policy carried out by the OECD from 1998-2000 shows that in a majority of countries there is significant unmet demand for provision. Participation by three year-olds varies very widely. In France, Belgium, Italy, Iceland and New Zealand, nearly all children of this age participate; in Germany, the Czech Republic and the United Kingdom some 50% participate; yet in Canada, Ireland, the Netherlands and Switzerland the participation rate is around 5% or less (OECD, 1999a).[6] Many challenges remain to fund and organise this first stage of lifelong learning in order to promote *quality* and *access* for all children and across all forms of provision.

...but clearly leave some demand unmet...

In some countries, there are certain populations with limited access to early childhood education and care: children from low-income families, children living in rural areas, and children with special needs. This raises serious equity issues. A range of different funding sources – public, private, business and parents – usually share the financing of early childhood education and care services. However, public investment by national and local government is a key factor in ensuring fair access for low-income families. Without a pro-active stance from the government, there is a large risk of a two-tiered system developing, with well-funded infrastructures for the upper income groups co-existing with poor-quality facilities and materials for children from low-income groups.

...and need particularly to think of underserved groups.

Encouraging adult learning

As noted in Figure 1.1 above, about two-thirds of the adult population in most countries do not participate in organised learning activities, measured over a twelve-month period (OECD and Statistics Canada, 2000). OECD work on the training of adult employees (OECD, 1999b) reveals significant differences between OECD countries in access to job-related training. More importantly, it shows, both within and between countries, that access to job-related training tends to reinforce existing inequalities in levels of educational attainment. This finding emphasises the importance of high levels of initial education, and of an equal distribution of levels of initial educational attainment, as a solid basis for encouraging wider participation by adults.

Adults too have uneven access, with the least educated participating least...

---

6. These data cover participation in only the formal and centre-based activities. Participation rates would likely be different if all early childhood education and care options were included. In the Netherlands, for example, around half of the 3 year-olds attend playgroups, and children at this age or younger are increasingly in day-care programmes. In England, 86% of 3 year-olds were enrolled in validated education programmes either in school or non-school settings and coverage is of a similar order in Scotland and Northern Ireland.

...and to address this, policy must address not just the nature of learning programmes, but the characteristics of workplaces.

Policies that can help motivate adults to learn were discussed in Section 6.2 above. How can the supply of learning opportunities, specifically in the workplace, be structured to improve access? Policies need to focus not just on specific characteristics of employee training programmes, but also on the organisation and structure of work and of enterprises, in ways that encourage competence-building and learning. Recent OECD work on knowledge management points out that learning need not be seen just as an accidental by-product of working life, but can be a deliberately engineered outcome of the ways in which organisations work. Learning-rich workplaces can be triggered in a number of ways: decentralised and flatter management structures; encouragement of employees to reflect upon their experiences; the use of team-based production; and through exposing workers to new problems in the production process (OECD, 2000*d*). Learning-rich workplaces are also stimulated by external factors such as an increasingly competitive business environment and by technological innovation (Smith, 2000). To the extent that these internal and external factors have been treated as matters of public policy, they have most typically fallen within the ambit of ministries of regional development, industry, technology or industrial relations. This observation serves to reiterate the importance of seeing lifelong learning as an integrated, and integrating, policy framework, and not just as a matter for education portfolios.

7.2 Diversity and access

More provision is not enough if it is not sensitive to diverse needs...

The increased diversity of learners, learning options and learner pathways poses challenges and opens up new approaches to address issues of access and equity. Evidence shows that expansion of education opportunities alone does not appear to reduce differences in participation rates between socio-economic groups (Chapter 3 of this volume). The segmentation across learning options, pathways and combinations is a major hurdle in meeting the diversity of learner needs and serves as a disincentive to participate. At tertiary-level studies, the ways in which standards are set and students are assessed appear inadequate to take in the very wide range of programme objectives, teaching methods and needs of individual students (OECD, 1998*a*).

...for example by adapting upper-secondary curricula...

Section 6.1 highlighted several approaches to strengthen the motivation to learn for the young by developing a range of pathways. Increased demand for a wider range of pathways has encouraged greater diversity at **upper secondary** level (OECD, 2000*a*). The OECD's work in this area has also highlighted the importance of making special provision for those having the greatest difficulty in coping with upper secondary education. This can be through a separate curriculum within the normal high school, specifically tailored to the weaker students, as in Sweden's Individual Programmes, in which some 11% of upper secondary students enrol. Or it can be through separate institutions with distinct pedagogical approaches, as in Denmark's Production Schools. In each case care is taken to ensure that the separate provision that is made for weaker students is not an educational dead-end, but provides opportunities for young people to rejoin the mainstream and complete an upper secondary qualification. In Australia, TAFE colleges (see Box 1.2 above), although not specifically designed for the weaker upper secondary students, are entered by many young people who leave upper secondary school early, and offer a more adult-centred learning environment that many young people find attractive.

Greater diversity of options also plays a role in **tertiary**-level participation. Some OECD countries – such as Canada and the United States – that have quite diverse tertiary education systems also have high levels of tertiary participation. Increased diversity can be achieved in many different ways: provision at non-university level; short-cycle degrees; vocationally-oriented university institutes; private-sector tertiary provision; expansion of distance learning and programme-level variation. Some OECD countries are giving priority to new forms of tertiary provision. For example, Hungary's tertiary education system introduced legislation in 1997 providing for the creation of new short-cycle accredited higher vocational education programmes intended to have a closer link to industry than traditional university courses. Sweden has taken similar steps, introducing short-cycle qualified vocational education tertiary courses in a 1996 pilot programme, that are open both to school leavers and those with work experience. Finland's 1992 reforms created polytechnics to provide more occupationally-oriented tertiary education, alongside the more theoretical and research-focused university qualifications. Mexico's new technological universities, similar to the French vocationally-oriented university institutes (IUTs), offer two-year, applied study courses aimed at labour market needs. Although recently introduced and still small in terms of numbers of institutions and students, the initial experience has been positive in terms of student quality and graduate employment. In the Czech Republic, 1998 legislation provides for more diverse tertiary education institutions and courses, although its implementation is still rather limited.

...and providing more options at tertiary level, such as short-cycle courses...

Another element of increased diversity of options is through wider study choices. The French IUTs provide study programmes with a greater emphasis on application. In addition, individual French universities are developing more distinctive profiles through the process of a contracting policy that provides funds to the institution on the basis of an institutional plan negotiated with the Ministry. Contracts specify agreed outcomes and may include partnerships with regional authorities, enterprises or other tertiary education institutions. Finland, which employs a similar contracting approach, allocates all funds through this means.

...and choices of more applied forms of study...

The growth of private tertiary education provision can offer another means of introducing greater diversity. Japan, Korea and the United States have large and diverse private sectors; in Mexico and Portugal, private-sector enrolment accounts for about one-fourth of the total. In many countries, public universities have established new corporate entities to ease and benefit from entry into a growing adult market for tertiary-level course modules, whether bearing academic credit or not. Other entrepreneurial corporate providers offering high-quality tertiary education now operate internationally as well as in national settings. The University of Phoenix, now the largest private university in the United States, offers degree studies in professional fields through learning sites located throughout the U.S. and internationally. Corporate provision in the IT field is now well-established (*e.g.* Microsoft, Sun Microsystems, Cisco), leading to certification on criteria set down by the industry (the counterpart of the involvement of professional bodies in advising on or setting degree standards in such fields as medicine, engineering, accountancy and law).

...along with more privately provided options...

...and an expansion of distance learning.

Distance education options have also expanded. Free-standing Open Universities in the United Kingdom, the Netherlands, Germany and Japan all serve clientele not easily reached by residential study options, including adults whose work or family responsibilities make attendance difficult or impossible. Traditional universities and further education colleges have expanded their own distance education provision, which in the mid-1990s still accounted for a larger share of non-residential enrolment than free standing institutions or other options. In an effort to harness the capacity of the region's institutions, the governors of the western US states established a virtual university, the Western Governors' University, to make available to learners in the region – and outside – the full range of study options and course modules across all of their state systems.

This has led to reconsideration of what makes a first degree.

At the programme level, there is considerable discussion on how the contents of the first tertiary-level qualification can be reshaped to provide a greater diversity of options. The Sorbonne/Bologna pan-European debate on a short first degree is an example of such discussions. In Denmark, Norway, Portugal, Germany and Finland (in the latter case, for a new formulation of the present long first degree), there is more discussion of vocational orientations of the first short degree. Likewise, there is support for better integration of general and specialised components of the bachelor's degree in Japan. Other approaches include encouraging or permitting various forms of cross-border, cross-segment and cross-level co-operation. Examples of these include franchising in the United Kingdom, specific linking arrangements in the United States and New Zealand, and joint degree programmes in the Netherlands.

8. RESOURCES FOR LIFELONG LEARNING

Investment in learning can pay off, if done carefully...

Investment in lifelong learning carries clear benefits, both economic and social (OECD, 1998b; OECD, 2000c). Public authorities wishing to implement lifelong learning strategies need to consider three aspects of resources. First, adequacy: are they *adequate* to support lifelong learning for different types and settings of provision and over different phases of life-cycle? Second, *efficiency*: are resources well used or are there efficiency gains to be reaped? Third, funding *sources*: if more resources are needed, who will pay for them and how can the resources be mobilised?

8.1 Adequacy and allocation of resources

...through adequate, well-allocated resources...

Whether or not current resources are adequate depends on how one interprets the goal of lifelong learning for all. The previous section on access and equity pointed to gaps in participation – see also Chapter 2 in this volume. Although many Member countries have set participation targets for individual sectors, none has set targets for the whole system of lifelong learning. Even if targets in each sector were identified, it would be extremely difficult to estimate the total costs involved in meeting them (OECD, 1999e).

Higher levels of participation will, in general, increase overall costs, but the magnitude of the increase will depend on a number of factors. The costs per unit of provision will be lower if existing available capacity can be used to cater to additional participants, as may be the case for distance learning.

Additional costs will be greater if the provision needed for the added participants must be organised in different ways, for example, to cater for poorly qualified adults. For some new patterns of lifelong learning, for example, part-time adult learning, the marginal costs may be lower than for the full-time studies in tertiary education. Despite the difficulty of developing precise cost estimates of different policy targets, it can be said with some confidence that even modest targets, taking the needs of young people as well as the adults into account, will require expansion in capacity (OECD, 1999e).[7] More resources will be needed if progress is to be achieved in reaching key goals: wider access to early childhood education and care, universal completion of upper secondary education, and greatly increased participation in adult learning.

8.2 Making more efficient use of resources

Greater efficiency in the use of existing resources offers one approach to meeting the demand for expanded learning opportunities. Member countries are using a variety of approaches to reduce the cost of provision and improve its quality. Efforts have been made in particular to cut teaching and personnel costs, to rationalise the structure of provision, to make better use of ICTs and to make more extensive use of the private sector.

...and by using resources efficiently...

Reducing teacher costs

The salaries of teachers and other personnel are the largest cost in the formal education system – on average they make up 82% of all current expenditure at the elementary and secondary levels and somewhat lower at the tertiary level. This proportion is increasing as the age profile of the teaching population rises. So any country that wants to make education systems more cost-effective must scrutinise teaching costs closely. A reduction in the number of young people entering secondary and tertiary education over the next few years does not necessarily reduce teaching costs in the short term. Teachers are often on permanent contracts and are not easily moved into areas where participation is rising, such as adult education.

...for example making best use of teaching resources...

OECD countries are pursuing a number of strategies to achieve savings in teaching and personnel costs (OECD, 1999e). Variants of higher student-teacher ratio have been used in Hungary, Italy, the Netherlands (during apprenticeship training), and Sweden (excepting upper secondary and special needs schools). Other approaches include restructuring the school system to reduce the number of teachers (Italy), reduced in-service training in school time (Austria), flexible contracts (Austria), reduced cost of sick leave and disability for staff (Netherlands), distance learning measures (Hungary, Japan and Norway) and greater use of teaching assistants in universities (Japan).

...through a variety of approaches...

---

7. Recent OECD work (OECD, 1999e) has estimated the expansion in capacity that would be required if participation rates were to rise to meet certain policy targets: at the pre-school level; for 15-19 year-olds; for 20-24 year-olds; and for adults. The analysis suggests that in many countries higher participation at the pre-school level and for 15-19 year-olds can be achieved with only a modest increase in resources. However, for 20-24 year-olds and for adults, higher participation rates would require a substantial expansion of capacity in many countries.

*...which must be balanced
with the need for quality.*

However, measures that cut teaching costs may conflict with the need to attract and maintain a high-quality teaching service. Many countries already find it more difficult to attract and retain younger teachers (Chapter 5 in this volume). They must strike a balance between reducing teaching costs and enhancing the quality of lifelong learning.

Rationalisation of provision

*Demography points to
rationalisation of school
provision...*

As a result of demographic trends, many countries are looking to rationalise their compulsory and upper secondary education systems and increase the funding available for other parts of the system (OECD, 2000*b*). The Netherlands, for example, has been involved in a "merger wave", which started in 1990. Since that date, a number of general secondary schools have merged to form larger comprehensive schools, in order to promote more efficient use of accommodation and equipment, and to reduce capital expenditure. In Austria, schools are reducing the number of lessons in some curriculum areas and limiting expenditure on textbooks.

*...while tertiary education
may be made more cost-
effective through increased
flexibility.*

In tertiary education, the approach can be described as a focus on making provision more flexible and responsive and, potentially, more cost-effective. The Czech Republic, the Netherlands and Sweden, for example, are focusing on the length of student programmes and are considering setting a fixed length of study time for degrees. In addition, Austria and the Netherlands are rationalising the number and type of courses on offer and, in some cases, the number of institutions where particular courses may be offered. Hungary is looking to increase the provision of courses that are shorter than traditional university degrees; Austria is improving the flexibility and speed of the processes required for the introduction of new courses. Both Austria and Hungary are increasingly introducing modular and individually tailored student programmes. One indication of inefficient use of resources, especially relevant for tertiary education, is the high non-completion rate. High drop-out rates are costly as they waste the efforts of students and institutional capacity and are detrimental to future participation in lifelong learning. To ensure student retention and achievement, provision must be more attractive and relevant. To this end, Austria has introduced an induction period for university students, which has helped to increase retention and to prevent costly course changes. Italy has required universities to check the background knowledge of incoming students in core subjects. The Netherlands has laid a greater emphasis on the selection and referral of students in the first phase of higher education to avoid high drop-out rates. Hungary is planning to rationalise university courses and institutions so that larger more comprehensive institutions will be more cost effective than a system of small, scattered and often specialist institutions. In Australia and Belgium (Flemish Community), a drive for effectiveness and quality motivated consolidation in tertiary education in the first half of the 1990s.

Comprehensive financing strategies are being used by several countries to promote efficiency as well as participation of adults. For example, policies to encourage improved efficiency seek to shift funding to an outcomes basis. The Danish "taximeter" approach is among the more innovative (see Box 1.3).

Box 1.3 **Danish taximeter system**

Under this scheme, funding for students is limited to the period of active engagement in study, which can occur in a continuous period without break or with stop-outs. Funding for institutions becomes available only when students pass their examinations. The scheme provides an incentive to providers to improve the efficiency of their programmes by allowing them to retain any excess in taximeter rates over the actual costs, and forcing them to pay any costs in excess of the taximeter rates. After several years of experience with the scheme, two issues of note have arisen:

– *The open-ended nature of the taximeter obligations.* Because the taximeter payments are guaranteed to approved institutions as long as they enrol students, it is possible, in principle, for them to enrol large numbers of persons, without limit. To address the budget uncertainty arising from this, the authorities agreed to create, from 1999, a reserve of 1-2% of the total allocation for the scheme to cover unforeseen surges in enrolments.

– *Inefficiencies arising from the gap between the actual cost of provision and the amount reimbursed by the taximeter scheme.* If the taximeter rates are adjusted too frequently to take account of efficiency gains, providers may have reduced incentive to pursue efficiency-enhancing innovations. If, on the other hand, taximeter rates are adjusted too slowly, there may be a loss in overall efficiency of the total expenditures to the extent that some providers continue to use less efficient methods. Although the ministry has no intention of recapturing the "profits" realised by those institutions whose actual costs are below the taximeter rates, there may be some adjustment in the rates to improve overall efficiency of the system.

The role of the private providers and competition

Many OECD countries are relying on expanded private capacity and increased competition in the provision of learning opportunities as a way to improve efficiency and to increase capacity. Japan has relied on private providers in all sectors of education and training for some time; the rapid expansion of participation in higher education could not have been achieved without this type of provision. Hungary and the Czech Republic have both passed legislation (in 1990 and 1998, respectively) to allow the establishment of private universities to help generate new capacity and encourage cost-effectiveness. The Danish Ministry of Labour relies entirely on outside, although government funded, providers for the provision of all its training and learning opportunities. Half are purchased from adult education providers supported by the Ministry of Education; the rest are purchased from technical/commercial colleges and business schools. Outcomes are certified in the same way, regardless of the provider. In Austria, authorities have developed a form of accreditation for local and foreign private institutions of higher education as a means of increasing the scope and scale of opportunities.

In many countries private provision plays a part in improving efficiency.

The use of ICTs for increasing cost-effectiveness

Information and communication technologies (ICTs) are seen by many OECD countries as among the most effective ways of increasing and widening participation in lifelong learning while keeping costs down to an affordable

Wider use of ICTs can keep costs down while widening opportunities.

level. Sweden's Forestry Project Initiative (Box 1.4), designed to address employers' needs for a more highly educated workforce, provides an example of how ICTs are being used to increase cost-effectiveness in the adult education sector. The study programme offered is considered to be more attractive than institutionally-based teaching programmes to potential participants, because they do not have to bear the costs of foregone earnings or accommodation costs often associated with more conventional educational provision. In addition, the contribution of the employers is lower than with conventional provision because they do not have to bear the cost of production losses. There is thus a greater incentive for both employees and employers to invest in this type of education.

Box 1.4 **Forestry project initiative in Sweden**

The aim of this project is to provide shift workers in the forestry industry with upper secondary level education in the core subjects of mathematics, chemistry, physics, Swedish and English. Tuition is carried out mainly through distance education and with the support of supervisors and new technology such as computers and interactive video. Education takes place mainly outside working hours, but in close proximity to learners' homes or workplaces.

Paper and pulp is a processing industry with production methods that are highly computerised and automated. Working as an operator imposes great demands on technical knowledge. Companies have great difficulty in recruiting personnel with a three-year upper secondary education, which in practice is the lowest theoretical educational background needed to manage the technology of the manufacturing process. Employees must also have good basic knowledge to acquire the necessary competence and technical education. By educating existing personnel in core subjects at the upper secondary level, the companies solve the problem of obtaining personnel with sufficient basic knowledge, at the same time as maintaining their existing skills.

Employees in the paper and pulp industry work shifts and have working hours which make it impossible for them to carry out part-time studies in traditional adult education. Socio-economic factors also make it more difficult for them to stay away from work and family too long. Moreover, longer absence from work would result in the loss of their current skills. This project is designed to address all these issues.

In January 1998, 12 paper mills were participating in the project and 231 employees were taking part. These mills are located all over Sweden and are typical of the industry in terms of capacity and number of employees. The project is managed by a steering group made up of a representative from the educational organisers, the employers and the industry's trade union.

A type of partnership approach between government, employers and individual learners underpins this project. The employers take responsibility for providing suitable premises for learning centres equipped with the necessary ICTs close to their factories. They are also responsible for paying supervisors. For its part, the government has granted SEK 1.4m per year over the three years of the project. The employees' side of the bargain is to be prepared to study outside working hours.

8.3 Mobilising new resources

There are strong incentives for investment in human capital for both individuals and the firms. Individuals with more education have better employment and pay prospects. The additional earning associated with tertiary education is higher than for completing upper secondary education. Enterprise-based training can produce gains to both individuals and firms. Dispersed evidence indicates that training does improve productivity, with about half the gain distributed in wages (OECD, 1999e). Over the 1990s, the private share in total financing of education increased, and a clear trend in favour of greater private contributions is visible in many OECD countries (OECD, 1999e). Private contributions are most prominent at the tertiary level, in the field of adult learning, and for early childhood education. Countries are experimenting with financing mechanisms that provide incentives for greater private investment in these areas. This section reviews some of the initiatives to promote wider private participation in financing tertiary-level studies and adult learning.

But expansion requires new resources to be mobilised, including from the private sector.

At **tertiary** level, there are a number of examples of innovative mechanisms to secure learner or third-party support: means-tested tuition fees in the United Kingdom, deferred, income-contingent and differential contributions in Australia. In New Zealand, tertiary tuition subsidies are available to all students irrespective of age or previous study.

Some countries are changing tuition fee systems...

New policies in the United Kingdom, France and the United States introduce new types of tertiary-level education eligible for funding. In the United Kingdom, Individual Learning Accounts (ILAs) are topped up with subsidies or discounts to help people undertake learning, from the public budget, and it is expected that most ILA-supported learners will choose among learning options through the services provided through *Learndirect* [the brand name of the University for Industry (UfI)], which is a brokering and information body (see Box 1.5). In the US, greatly expanded tax breaks for education now allow learners to deduct from their taxes part of the costs of tertiary education studies. Learners

...or widening the types of tertiary study eligible for public support...

Box 1.5 **Use of new technologies**

The University for Industry (UfI) in the United Kingdom is a new initiative to provide a national on-line and distributed learning network. It became operational in Autumn 2000. It is intended to be a new kind of organisation, working in partnership with the public, private and voluntary sectors, to promote and broker open and distance learning. The objectives are to stimulate demand for lifelong learning amongst businesses and individuals and promote the availability of, and improve access to, relevant, high-quality and innovative learning, in particular through the use of ICTs.

Using modern digital technologies, the UfI brokers high-quality learning products/services and makes them available at home, in the workplace and in a network of *Learndirect* centres countrywide. It aims to break down barriers to learning by making provision more flexible and accessible, by stimulating new markets to bring down costs, by offering clear, reliable information and advice and by providing opportunities for people to learn at their own pace and in convenient locations. It will promote learning ranging from the basic skills of literacy and numeracy to specialised technological skills and business management.

enrolling for as little as one course module, in a wide variety of tertiary education institutions, may claim the credit.

...but adult education remains of low funding priority, with some exceptions.

Funding for **general adult education** is often precarious. It tends to receive low priority in central government education budgets and local funding can be subject to the vagaries of local government financial situations. Public funding systems often lack efficiency incentives and there tend to be few mechanisms for monitoring the quality or benefits of adult education provision. One interesting example is Denmark where most of the direct costs of adult education and training are borne by the state, or regional or local authorities, through the taximeter payments and other forms of institutional support. Individuals and enterprises pay a lesser portion of the direct costs. For example, 60% of the Folk High Schools' revenues come from the state, with the balance from individuals and private companies. Student fees pay 20–40% of the costs for Open Education courses. In the adult vocational training programmes operated by labour market authorities, the share paid by enterprises for their employees ranges from nothing, for training that uses standard courseware, to 100% for training that uses tailor-made curricula. Where a trainee allowance is paid by the state (in cases where training leave for employed workers is not paid), the employer pays a share calculated in the same way (up to 100% for tailor-made courses).

9. POLICY CO-ORDINATION

OECD reviews have demonstrated the need for co-ordination among stakeholders – in provision for adults, for young children and for young people in transition.

As lifelong learning involves stakeholders beyond education ministries – learners and their families, institutional and other providers, and social partners – co-ordination in policy development and implementation is essential for success. The thematic reviews conducted by the OECD during its current mandate have highlighted both the challenges of co-ordination and successful initiatives countries have taken in addressing them. The thematic review of early childhood education and care policies puts emphasis on co-ordinating education, health, social and family policies in providing access to quality education and care services for all children. The thematic review of adult learning emphasises the close interaction that is required between education, training, labour market and social policies in meeting the needs of adult learners. This section uses examples from the thematic review of the transition from initial education to working life (OECD, 2000a) to illustrate some of the challenges of co-ordination and lessons for policy.

The case of young people in transition illustrates particularly powerfully...

The transition review illustrates a wide range of experiences on how countries are attempting to solve co-ordination challenges:

– Through different ministries and agencies working together;

– Through the involvement of employers, trade unions and other actors in policy development nationally and in programme delivery locally;

– Through community involvement in local policy development and programme implementation.

Based on these experiences, four conclusions can be drawn about the relationship between policy development and programme implementation processes on the one hand, and some key labour market and educational outcome indicators such as employment rates and qualification attainments on the other.

First, in those countries in which different government portfolios harmonise their policies, and co-ordinate their claims upon public resources, some of the more difficult transition problems that young people experience can be addressed more readily. For example in Norway and Sweden there is broad agreement that young people under the age of 20, and in Denmark, those under the age of 18, shall be the responsibility of local authorities, and hence primarily of the education system, rather than of the public employment service. This has enabled clear agreement to be reached that the principal goal in assisting early school leavers should be school re-entry so that an upper secondary qualification can be gained. It prevents education and labour competing for funds targeted at young people at risk in the labour market. And it prevents the placement of poorly qualified early school leavers in low-skilled and insecure jobs being used as a success measure in judging policy effectiveness. These policies are associated with low, and declining, rates of long-term unemployment for those under the age of 20 in these countries.

…that co-operation between ministries pays off…

Second, countries with nationally-negotiated collective agreements tend to experience better transition outcomes than do those countries in which such matters are more typically left to local and individual discretion. These national agreements affect many of the key arrangements to aid young people's post-school transitions – work-related curriculum, certification arrangements, wage rates, employer roles and responsibilities – which are set out, often at the level of the industry, between governments, employers, and most typically trade unions. Both in strong apprenticeship countries like Germany and Switzerland and in others such as Denmark and Norway where apprenticeship plays a smaller role, positive outcomes for young people are associated with strong involvement by the social partners in setting the frame-works for youth transition – in vocational schools, in career guidance and in labour market programmes.

…that nationally-negotiated agreements can play a useful role…

Third, in such countries, close involvement of the key partners is not simply evident in policy development. It can also be observed in the on-going implementation of these frameworks: in helping to assure quality through selection of students and employers; in assessment of students; in curriculum revision. This is a particular feature of apprenticeship arrangements in Austria, Denmark, Germany, Norway and Switzerland. It can also be observed in the strong role played by employers and the trade unions in the day-to-day management of the technical, agricultural and commercial colleges that form the backbone of Denmark's vocational education system for youth.

…that day-to-day co-operation enhances policy-level agreements…

Finally, this involvement extends beyond the national level to the local and regional levels. Countries that experience good transition outcomes for their youth generally do not simply leave all of the action to national peak bodies. Extensive involvement of employers, trade unions, and communities can be seen at the local level: in providing career guidance and career information; in making local safety nets for early leavers work; in local work experience and community service projects. In Austria, for example,

…and lastly the importance of local-level co-operation…

employers and trade unions have a strong involvement at the local level in providing career information and advice to young people. In Norway, local employer organisations host training circles that allow resources for apprenticeship training to be more widely accessed by small and medium-sized enterprises.

...but emulating successful countries is difficult, because there are many pieces to the jigsaw...

Many countries that have had less effective transition outcomes have been inspired by these examples, and in some cases have tried to copy some of their features. Often this copying, for example, of the German-speaking countries' dual system of apprenticeship, has been less than successful, because only some parts of the jigsaw – national co-operation in policy development, the involvement of the parties in programme implementation, or local initiatives that involve the partners – have been adopted, but not other key ingredients. Part of the difficulty in adopting the policy and implementation frameworks observed in countries with successful transition outcomes is institutional; *e.g.* the lack of well-organised national employer bodies with a strong network of regional branches.

...however some countries have been able to improve the institutional frameworks.

Nevertheless, some countries have shown that institutions can be subject to major reforms, and effective new institutions can be created. For example, five decades ago, Japan increased schools responsibility for graduate job placement in co-operation with the national Public Employment Security Office. The strong relationships between schools and firms that this has encouraged have been a key explanation for the effectiveness of its transition outcomes for youth. In the 1990s, Hungary, in introducing a modern framework for vocational and educational training to replace the system linked to former state-owned enterprises, passed legislation to require compulsory membership of employers' chambers, and gave these bodies powers over apprenticeship quality control that closely matched those in German-speaking countries. Australia, for example, has put in place a large national programme – the Jobs Pathway Programme – to help connect employers and schools and further education institutions. This programme has much in common with the relationship between schools and firms observed in Japan. Several countries are taking steps to develop new institutional frameworks for the transition that suit their own national circumstances. The experience of the transition review shows that governments have an important role to play in co-operation with others in making such change possible. In Australia and the United States, for example, governments have played a strong role in attempting to stimulate strong local partnerships between firms and schools. The Australian government has created a national independent yet government-funded body – the Australian Student Traineeship Foundation – to stimulate these partnerships and help to improve their quality. Australian experience has shown that such national government support can be an important stimulus provoking employer organisations to begin developing frameworks to support local initiatives. In the United States, the 1994 School-to-Work Opportunities Act provided funds for the stimulation of local and regional partnerships between school and employers. Canada's experience has shown that, without such clear government support, workplace learning partnerships for youth in transition are far more fragile.

10. CONCLUSIONS

This review shows that there are grounds for optimism and grounds for caution in assessing the delivery of lifelong learning in OECD countries. The optimism arises from the fact that many pieces of the lifelong learning jigsaw can already be widely observed in OECD countries. The caution arises from the fact that no country has yet put them together to complete the jigsaw.

Too often the pieces of the lifelong learning jigsaw remain unconnected...

In 1996, OECD Education Ministers articulated a "cradle-to-grave" vision of lifelong learning that was substantially broader than the notions of adult education or recurrent education that had tended to shape debates on lifelong learning up to that point. This review shows that the broader concept has been embraced at the political level. But at the level of practical policy development and implementation, responses have neither been consistent nor uniform. There is little evidence of wholehearted pursuit of lifelong learning strategies at the *system* level, for example through setting system-wide policy targets. The progress that has been made is in moulding reforms in various sectors of provision in the context of lifelong learning and the systemic demands that it brings. But again this is not uniform either across sectors, within a country or across countries.

...as policy responses have been neither consistent nor uniform across learning systems.

What is needed to give greater vitality to the notion of lifelong learning for all, therefore, are reforms that make learning throughout the lifecycle work better as a system, so that the whole is greater than the sum of the parts. This is true in each of the five areas of focus highlighted in this chapter.

To make lifelong learning work better as a system, countries need:

First, **assessment and recognition mechanisms** have in many countries been improved in various encouraging ways, for example, by giving credit for various informal courses, by allowing students to follow certain pathways that were hitherto impossible, and by starting in some cases to provide better information about courses. A whole-system approach would aim to create a connected network of opportunities. Credit would be given, and courses made visible, according to their content and outcomes rather than to where they happened to take place. To move in this direction, countries need to make a principle of removing any unwarranted institutional barriers to learners taking up and getting credit for learning activities.

...to make learning opportunities hang together as a coherent network...

Second, **foundations for learning** are being strengthened for young people and for adults, in particular in countries that recognise the importance of improving people's motivation in the first instance to engage in organised learning and thereafter to become self-driven learners. There are numerous examples of measures to increase the relevance of learning at school (particularly to under-achieving groups) and others that make adult learning more enjoyable or more structured around adults' distinctive needs. Yet countries have not explicitly put motivation and engagement at the centre of their educational foundations, which remain oriented to processing students through recognised educational stages. A systemic rethinking of the foundation would require basic curriculum goals to be fundamentally readjusted, to emphasise the creation of lifelong competency and inclination to learn, as much as current mastery of the curriculum.

...to put motivation and engagement in learning at the heart of basic education...

Third, old principles of **equity and access** are being applied in new ways. There remain some significant gaps in the quantity of provision. In response, some countries are recognising the importance, for example, of widening access to

...to extend learning to all by making it an inclusive part of the culture...

... not just by making more places available...

early childhood education. However, access is not just a matter of quantity of places or courses, but of the nature of the opportunities and of the wider context in which they are offered. At work, creating a learning-rich environment can be as important to learning as the number of training courses that are offered. In tertiary education, unless expansion is matched by a greater diversity of learning options, it may serve primarily already-privileged groups. So equity needs to involve an inclusive approach to all aspects of learning in society, not just a political decision to expand provision to fill gaps.

...to look at optimal ways of deploying resources, looking across sectors...

Fourth, while more **resources** have been made available during the 1990s, they still do not match burgeoning demand. This is partly a quantitative issue – more would be needed overall to fill gaps in provision – but also a matter of how to deploy resources wisely and how to muster private as well as public sources. These questions are being asked in individual sectors, but the efficiency of the system as a whole is not being addressed. A systemic approach would go further than most governments have so far dared, and ask whether the allocation of resources across different sectors of provision and over the lifetime is optimal from a social and economic point of view. Both the benefits and the costs of learning need to be evaluated over the lifetime. Existing data are, however, extremely limited for this evaluation, particularly because little is known about expenditure outside the formal education sector.

...and lastly to ensure that working together in partnership to these ends becomes a priority, not just rhetoric

Finally, **policy co-ordination** is today widely preached and selectively practiced. In policies to improve young people's transitions, for example, a number of countries have strong traditions of working across agencies, including with organisations outside government. But what is harder is establishing such co-operative arrangements where such traditions do not exist. Some attempts at copying arrangements from other countries have not worked well. Each country needs to look at its own context, and consider carefully what is the best way to break down existing cultural divides that hinder collaboration. Having accepted that lifelong learning is too wide an enterprise to be left to any one agency or ministry, OECD societies need to make a priority of working together to make it a reality. ∎

References

BERNARD VAN LEER FOUNDATION (1994), *Why Children Matter: Investing in Early Childhood Care and Development*, Den Haag, The Netherlands.

BJØRNÅVOLD, J. (2000), *Making Learning Visible: Assessment and Recognition of Non-Formal Learning in Europe*, CEDEFOP, Thessaloniki, Greece.

CANDY, P. and **CREBART, R.** (1997), "Australia's Progress towards Lifelong Learning", *Comparative Studies on Lifelong Learning Policies*, NIER and UIE, Tokyo, Japan.

CENTRAL COUNCIL FOR EDUCATION (1981), *On Lifelong Integrated Education*, Tokyo, Japan.

COLARDYN, D. (1996), *La gestion des compétences*, Presses Universitaires de France, Paris.

COLLEGE BOARD (1978), *Lifelong Learning during Adulthood, An Agenda for Research: Future Directions for a Learning Society*, College Entrance Examination Board, New York, United States.

COUNCIL OF MINISTERS OF EDUCATION CANADA, (1999), *Report on Public Expectations of Postsecondary Education in Canada*.

DEETYA – DEPARTMENT FOR EMPLOYMENT, EDUCATION, TRAINING AND YOUTH AFFAIRS (1998), *Learning for Life: Review of Higher Education Financing and Policy*, Social Report, Canberra, Australia.

DELCI, M. (1997), "Lifelong Learning in the United States", *Learning to Monitor Lifelong Learning*, Working Paper prepared for the OECD, NCRVE, University of California, Berkeley, United States.

DEPARTMENT FOR EDUCATION AND EMPLOYMENT (1998), *The Learning Age: A Renaissance for a New Britain*, Green Paper submitted to the Parliament, February, London, United Kingdom.

DEPARTMENT OF EDUCATION AND SCIENCE (2000), *Learning for Life: White Paper on Adult Education*, July, Dublin, Ireland.

MINISTRY OF EDUCATION (1997), *The Joy of Learning: A National Strategy for Lifelong Learning*, Committee Report, No. 14, Helsinki, Finland.

MINISTRY OF EDUCATION, CULTURE AND SCIENCE (1998), *Lifelong Learning: The Dutch Initiative*, Den Haag, The Netherlands.

MINISTRY OF EDUCATION, RESEARCH AND CHURCH AFFAIRS (2000), *The Competence Reform in Norway*, Plan of Action 2000-2003, Oslo, Norway.

NATIONAL AGENCY FOR EDUCATION (2000), *Lifelong Learning and Lifewide Learning*, January, Stockholm, Sweden.

OECD (1998a), *Redefining Tertiary Education*, Paris.

OECD (1998b), *Human Capital Investment: An International Comparison*, CERI, Paris.

OECD (1998c), *Co-ordinating Services for Children and Youth at Risk: A World View*, CERI, Paris.

OECD (1999a), "Early Childhood Education and Care: Getting the most from the investment", *Education Policy Analysis*, CERI, Paris.

OECD (1999b), "Training of Adult Workers in OECD Countries: Measurement and analysis", *Employment Outlook*, Paris.

OECD (1999c), *Measuring Student Knowledge and Skill: A New Framework for Assessment*, PISA, Paris.

OECD (1999d), "Tertiary education: Extending the benefits of growth to new groups", *Education Policy Analysis*, CERI, Paris.

OECD (1999*e*), "Resources for Lifelong Learning: what might be needed and how might it be found", *Education Policy Analysis*, CERI, Paris.

OECD (1999*f*), *Inclusive Education at Work: Students with Disabilities in Mainstream Schools*, CERI, Paris.

OECD (1999*g*), *Overcoming Exclusion through Adult Learning*, CERI, Paris.

OECD (2000*a*), *From Initial Education to Working Life: Making Transitions Work*, Paris.

OECD (2000*b*), "Making Lifelong Learning Affordable", Synthesis report based on 11 country submissions.

OECD (2000*c*), *Motivating Students for Lifelong Learning*, CERI, Paris.

OECD (2000*d*), *Knowledge Management in the Learning Society*, CERI, Paris.

OECD (2001), *The Well-being of Nations: the role of human and social capital*, CERI, Paris.

OECD and **STATISTICS CANADA** (2000), *Literacy in the Information Age: Final Report of the International Adult Literacy Survey*, Paris.

PRESIDENTIAL COMMISSION ON EDUCATIONAL REFORM (1996), *Education Reform for a New Education System: To Meet the Challenges of Information and Globalisation Era*, Seoul, Republic of Korea.

SMITH, A. (2000), "Industry Training in Australia: Causes and Consequences", paper delivered to a conference on Vocational training and lifelong learning in Australia and Germany, May, Potsdam, Germany.

STATISTICS CANADA AND COUNCIL OF MINISTERS OF EDUCATION CANADA (2000), *Education Indicators in Canada 1999*.

UNESCO (1997), ISCED1997 – *International standard classification of education*, Paris.

U.S. DEPARTMENT OF EDUCATION and **OECD** (1999), *How Adults Learn*, Proceedings of a conference held April 6-8, 1998, Georgetown University Conference Centre, Washington, D.C.

WOLF, A. (1995), *Competence-Based Assessment*, Open University Press, Buckingham, United Kingdom.

chapter 2

LIFELONG LEARNING FOR ALL: TAKING STOCK

SUMMARY

It is difficult to evaluate the implementation of lifelong learning because strategies vary across countries and measuring implementation is complex. This chapter takes stock by constructing indicators on the basis of the best available international data.

Indicators examine how the *foundations of learning* are being strengthened, in terms of: access to education in early childhood; the proportion of persons in successive generations that completes upper secondary education, where there is a marked trend towards near-universal completion; the quality of upper-secondary education as gauged by the literacy levels of recent completers; and the proportion of persons in successive generations that completes tertiary education, where differences remain in spite of rapid growth.

Further indicators look at *learning opportunities for adults*, in terms of: the proportion of students who are adults, where few countries have more than a tiny percentage; the amount of education and training that adults undertake; and the literacy levels achieved by older adults with a given level of initial education.

Two indicators take stock of the *affordability of lifelong learning*, in terms of: trends in per-student costs and enrolments; and the growth in public and private spending on learning activities. On both measures, the picture is mixed by education level and across countries.

Overall, few countries do well on the majority of measures; most have mixed performance. The few countries spending the most on learning appear to do the best; for others, there is no apparent relationship between public spending and lifelong learning.

1. INTRODUCTION

The mandate to make lifelong learning a reality for all was inspired by the need to ensure that all individuals have the knowledge, skills and competencies to participate fully in a knowledge-based society. Chapter 1 shows that the mandate implies for many countries a fairly radical transformation of existing formal and informal settings in which learning occurs if they are to serve as a tool for inclusion rather than selection and to put the individual at the centre of the learning process.

That being the case, it is important to monitor the *implementation* of lifelong learning across Member countries. This immediately raises the question of which criteria should be used to monitor implementation. Presently, few countries specify objectives against which it would be possible to evaluate progress. This chapter seeks to fill the void by monitoring developments in Member countries with respect to two broad objectives in the mandate: *a*) strengthening foundation and continuing learning and *b*) increasing the affordability of lifelong learning. It does this on the basis of a number of indicators that are calculated using the best available international comparable data, and that cover the main sectors in which lifelong learning occurs: early childhood education and care, schools, tertiary education institutions, the workplace and other adult learning settings.

The chapter proceeds as follows. Section 2 sets out the approach used to examine country performance and its limitations. Section 3 presents indicators of country performance on foundation and further learning, followed by a section considering country performance on indicators of financing lifelong learning. Section 5 assesses overall country performance in realising lifelong learning. The final section draws together the main conclusions of this stocktaking exercise and offers suggestions on how to improve the monitoring of lifelong learning.

2. TAKING STOCK OF WHERE COUNTRIES STAND: A SYSTEMIC APPROACH

A stocktaking of country performance on lifelong learning is not straightforward. First, as Chapter 1 makes clear, lifelong learning is not defined solely in terms of discrete policies or institutions with specific missions. The lifelong learning mandate superimposes new objectives – extending learning to younger ages and ensuring sound foundations for learning for everyone – on pre-existing education, training, and learning sectors. Moreover, the mandate is being implemented at a time when various sectors are undergoing important transformations – rising participation in early childhood education, increased permeability of the boundaries between post-secondary pathways, and qualitative and quantitative changes in tertiary education. Some of these transformations have preceded or occurred independently of policies whose stated aim is to further lifelong learning.

Stocktaking is complicated also by the fact that lifelong learning is most clearly defined in terms of learning by individuals rather than by inputs into institutions. While lifelong learning strategies should be evaluated in terms of outcomes for individuals, such evaluations are hindered because many variables are likely to intervene between lifelong learning policies and individual outcomes. Furthermore, on a practical level, internationally comparable data on learning outcomes are limited and recent. Coverage of the wide range of competencies associated with lifelong learning remains partial, and cross-sectional time-series or longitudinal data do not exist on most dimensions of interest. Mindful of these constraints, this chapter draws on available international education and training indicators from Indicators of National Education Systems (INES) and the International Adult Literacy Survey (IALS) to paint a picture of the present state of lifelong learning in OECD countries.

3. STRENGTHENING FOUNDATION AND FURTHER LEARNING

A prerequisite for lifelong learning is a sound foundation in basic educational competencies acquired in the formal education system and opportunities for further learning once persons leave initial education and training. There is ample evidence that, on average, children are more likely to under-perform in compulsory education if they enter school poorly prepared to learn (OECD, 1999a, Chapter 2). Students do badly in tertiary-level studies if they lack critical analytical and drafting skills (OECD, 1998a). Adults who are unable to read can hardly learn on the job or benefit from further training (OECD and Statistics Canada, 2000) or overcome the risk of social exclusion in a knowledge-based society (U.S. Department of Education and OECD, 1999). Further learning by the adult population is associated with better jobs and working conditions, and with improved enterprise performance (OECD, 1997; OECD, 1999b, Chapters 3 and 4).

A solid foundation is crucial for further learning.

Better basic learning depends on expanding participation in a range of learning activities as well as raising their quality. Lifelong learning opportunities for adults are more difficult to assess because they cut across formal and non-formal arrangements. Based on available evidence on the quantity and quality of learning, the indicators presented below enable a partial assessment of where countries stand with respect to strong education foundations and overall learning opportunities for adults.

3.1 Early childhood education and care (ECEC)

There is no doubt about the importance of the early childhood period in the cognitive, behavioural, and social development of children, and in developing a sound foundation for lifelong learning. Disadvantages at this stage of life can hinder later learning. But what this implies for policy depends on societal views as to the respective roles of society at large and the family. Some countries opt for policies that reinforce the role of the family by making it easier for a working parent to withdraw from the workforce for a period to care for children at home. This alleviates the need for extra capacity in institutional settings for early childhood education and care. Other countries emphasise creating ECEC programmes for children whose parents work. Policies in other countries are neutral with respect to incentives to favour early childhood development and care in the home or in institutional settings. In order to make an assessment of progress on this front, it would be helpful to know the proportion of young children who are at home with a parent, or are participating in an organised care and development programme; it would be even better to complement this with data on participation rates of children

Countries differ in how they define and meet the needs of young children. Many, though not all countries, are committed to making pre-primary care widely available.

from disadvantaged families or families in which parents work. It would be helpful to know how much governments allocate for young children, either in the form of support for opportunities in various institutional settings, or in the form of transfers to families who keep their children at home until the beginning of compulsory education. Ideally, we would want to complement data on participation rates with some information on the quality of the experience of children, whether at home or in an institutional setting. But this raises the thorny question of how to define quality and how to assess what is happening with young children at home as well as in a variety of institutional settings.

Differences in the percentage of 3-year-olds enrolled in such activities reflect real differences in policies and practices…

A more limited and pragmatic approach is to review the existing range of international indicators on ECEC and to interpret such data with due regard to other considerations such as evidence on whether parents are likely to be able to assume full-time child-care responsibilities themselves. One such indicator is the proportion of three-year olds served in pre-primary education programmes. Figure 2.1 shows a very dispersed pattern across OECD countries with respect to provision of learning opportunities for three-year olds in 1998, ranging from over 90% in France, Belgium (Flemish Community) and Italy to less than 5% in Ireland and Turkey. The OECD thematic review on early childhood education and care suggests that there are limitations to this particular indicator.

Figure 2.1 Participation in pre-primary education[1] for children aged 3, 1998

In some countries, nearly all 3-year-olds participate in pre-primary education; in others, less than half do so.

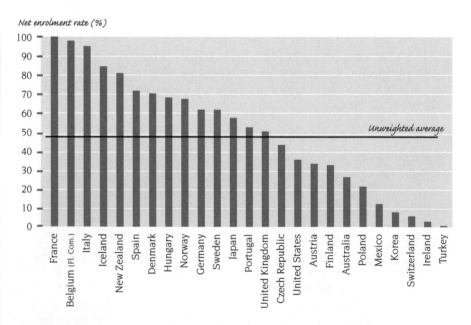

Net enrolment rate (%)

1. The data refer to participation in organised centre-based instruction programmes primarily covering children aged 3 to compulsory school age. Programmes organised as day care, play groups and home-based structured and developmental activities are not included, and participation in programmes organised through health or social welfare ministries or privately are not, in all countries, reported.

Source: OECD (2000), *Education at a Glance – OECD Indicators*, Chart C1.2. ....
Data for Figure 2.1, p. 145.

For example, in Australia and some other countries there are significant options for care that are organised outside the context of those institutional providers whose enrolments are captured in the statistics. Countries which have opted to emphasise ECEC activities within the family do not show high participation rates on this measure. Despite these limitations, much of the variation seen in Figure 2.1 reflects real differences in policies and priorities. For example, the differences in participation rates are partly a reflection of the evident policy choices regarding the allocation of financial resources. Those enrolling more than a half of all three-year-olds in organised centre-based programmes typically spend more than 0.5% of GDP on pre-primary education *e.g.* France spends 0.7% and Denmark spends 1.1%.

What does this evidence about pre-primary education imply for the state of lifelong learning? First, probably more than in any other area of learning, it is difficult to discern a norm or "best practice". The variance across countries in participation rates and overall spending appears to reflect a high degree of differentiation in policies. The OECD's thematic review of early childhood education and care has found considerable variation across countries with respect to the age of eligibility for publicly-provided programmes, and the extent to which they are targeted or universal. Countries also differ with respect to the degree that such services are centrally administered and regulated, and the extent to which ancillary policies, such as provisions for parental leave, are related to ECEC policies (OECD, 1999*a*, Chapter 2). In Europe, countries differ in the nature of the institutions that provide ECEC. Nearly all except the Nordic countries rely on nurseries/day-care/play groups for children up to age 3; the Nordics rely on non-school education-oriented programmes; Spain has school-based programmes that begin at less than 6 months. Arrangements become less diverse within countries and across countries starting at the age of three, the age at which participation in some countries rises markedly. Three-fourths of all EU countries rely entirely or partly on schools; half rely on mixtures of two or more forms of provision (European Commission, 2000, pp. 43-63).

... and make it difficult to discern "best practice".

In sum, it appears that ECEC is one of the biggest unfinished items on the agenda for implementing lifelong learning. Estimates suggest that, for most countries for which data are available, capacity would need to increase substantially on its 1995 base (*e.g.* by more than 20%), if participation rates of all children below the age of 6 are to reach by 2005 the levels found in the countries with the highest participation rates. Switzerland, Finland, and Turkey, for example, would need to increase capacity by 100% or more to achieve these levels (OECD, 1999*a*, Chapter 1, Figure 1.2).

3.2 Upper secondary education and training

Perhaps the most important element of a sound foundation for lifelong learning is ensuring that young persons leave the formal education system with at least the minimum qualifications required for employability and access to further training. Recent OECD research suggests that, on average, completion of upper secondary education or acquiring a recognised apprenticeship certificate marks the minimum threshold for successful entry into the labour market and continuing employability (OECD, 1998*b*; OECD, 2000*a*; OECD and Statistics Canada, 2000).

Completion of upper secondary education or apprenticeship is a minimum condition for a foundation for lifelong learning...

... and nearly all countries have achieved this for a large majority of young persons...

The good news on this front is that Member countries are now converging on high – even near-universal – completion of upper secondary education. Figure 2.2 shows that in nearly two-thirds of Member countries, 70% or more of 25 to 29 year-olds in 1998 had completed upper secondary education. In the Czech Republic, Norway and Korea, more than 90% of this age group has completed upper secondary education.

... in some countries following dramatic improvements of attainment levels.

There has been broad progress over the past 25 years in raising upper secondary education completion rates. Figure 2.2 puts current attainment levels in perspective by comparing the attainment levels of 25-29 year olds today, to those of 50-54 year-olds who left school two to three decades ago. Some of the most dramatic improvements, *e.g.* in Spain and Portugal, have occurred in countries where past levels of educational attainment were very low. Countries such as Australia, France, Korea, and Finland have almost caught up with the countries having the highest upper secondary completion rates.

Figure 2.2 | Progress towards achieving a minimum educational attainment level, 1998

Percentages of 25-29 year-olds and 50-54 year-olds who have completed upper secondary education

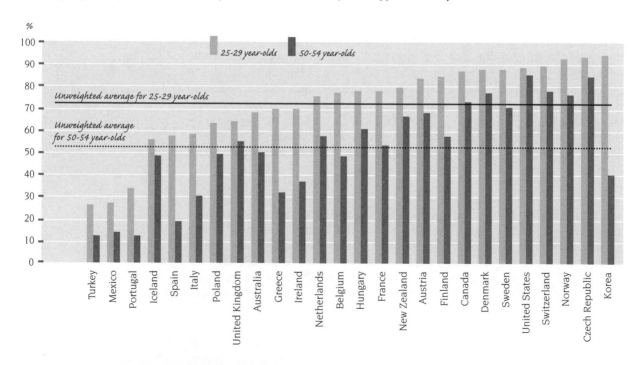

Young adults are more likely than older adults to have completed upper secondary education; the improvement has been greatest in countries where older adults have the least education.

Countries are ranked in ascending order, by attainment level of 25-29 year-olds.

Source: OECD Labour Force Survey Database (2000). ....

Data for Figure 2.2, p. 145.

As noted above, strategies for lifelong learning also need to be evaluated in terms of the *quality* of learning outcomes. In this regard, some countries face substantial challenges not simply to raise or sustain participation rates, but also to improve the quality of outcomes. The OECD thematic review on the transition from initial education to working life suggests a number of additional indicators that might be used to evaluate how well countries are addressing the quality issue. One proxy measure for this is mean literacy scores, as measured by the International Adult Literacy Survey (IALS).[1] of young persons who have completed upper secondary education. Another proxy measure of quality is the "under-achievement rate", the proportion of upper secondary education completers whose performance on literacy tasks is below the minimum level of competence needed, as judged by experts, to cope adequately with the complex demands of everyday life (below level 3) (OECD, 1997). Figure 2.3 presents data on these two proxy measures of quality. The mean literacy level for upper secondary completers aged 16-25 is represented by the vertical bars;

But the quality of secondary education is variable across countries.

Figure 2.3 Literacy scores[1] and under-achievement rates[2] of population aged 16-25 with upper secondary education, 1994-98

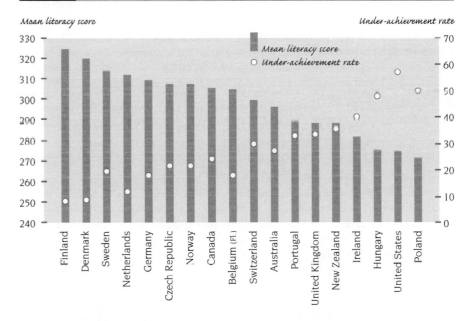

Mean literacy score — *Under-achievement rate*

Legend: Mean literacy score / Under-achievement rate

1. Document scale, with range of 0-500 points.
2. Percentage performing below literacy level 3 (275 or below) on document scale.

Countries are ranked in descending order by mean literacy score.

Source: International Adult Literacy Survey Database; OECD and Statistics Canada (2000), *Literacy in the Information Age*, Table 3.5. ....
Data for Figure 2.3, p. 145.

People who complete secondary education have very different literacy levels. The average proportion with low literacy ranges from 10% to nearly 60%.

---

1. Literacy levels of individuals were assessed in 18 countries, between 1994 and 1998 using the International Adult Literacy Survey (IALS). Survey participants provided information on educational attainment, other background characteristics, and employment and training experience. For more information on the definitions and measurement of literacy, and the results of the survey, see OECD (1997) and OECD and Statistics Canada (2000).

values are read off the left-hand axis. The under-achievement rate for each country, is indicated by a circle; its value is read off the right-hand axis. The data show that there is considerable variation across countries with respect to mean literacy scores of upper secondary completers, with mean scores in Finland and Denmark just below literacy level 4 (326-375), and mean scores in Poland and the United States at the top of literacy level 2 (226-275). There is substantially more variation with respect to "under-achievement" rates. In Finland, less than 10% of persons who have completed upper secondary education fail to reach literacy at level 3 (threshold score of 276), while in the United States, nearly 59% do. Mean literacy scores of 16-25 year old completers are loosely correlated with completion rates (see Figure 2.2). There are some notable exceptions, though. The United States with one of the highest upper secondary completion rates has the second lowest mean literacy score. In contrast, Portugal, with one of the lowest completion rates of the countries considered, has a mean literacy score that is only slightly below the mean for all countries.

3.3 Tertiary education

Opportunities for tertiary education need to be widely available.

As completion of upper secondary education has become near-universal, participation in tertiary education has come to be viewed as an important prerequisite for working and further learning throughout adult life. The criteria for evaluating and comparing country performance in this area are not as clear-cut as they are in the case of upper secondary education because it is difficult to identify appropriate benchmarks for participation rates and programmes of study.

Overall, Canada, Japan, and the United States have the highest proportion of persons with tertiary qualifications ...

The most obvious variable to monitor in taking stock of this dimension of lifelong learning is the proportion of the population with tertiary qualifications. Such measures show marked differences across countries ranging from 15% or less of adults aged 25-64 in countries, such as Austria, the Czech Republic, Hungary, Italy, and Portugal, to more than 30% in Canada, Japan, and the United States (OECD, 2000a, p. 33). However, as countries have pursued policies in the 1980s and 1990s to expand participation in tertiary education, it is more telling to examine recent trends in participation and the relative emphasis on academic versus more applied and technical streams of study in tertiary education.

... but most countries are catching up ...

One way to do this is to compare the proportion of 30-34 year-olds with tertiary qualifications with the proportion of 50-54 year-olds with similar qualifications. Attainment of tertiary qualifications has increased in those countries where the attainment rate of the younger group exceeds that of the older group. Such data are presented in Figure 2.4, where countries are ranked in ascending order of attainment rates of the younger group. There is a large spread across countries in terms of how quickly lagging countries are catching up with the leaders. In Greece, Iceland, Korea and Spain, 30-34 year-olds are more than twice as likely as 50-54 year-olds to have acquired tertiary qualifications. Of these countries, all but Greece have had increases large enough to raise attainment of the younger group above the OECD average. However, for most countries with available data, the proportions

Figure 2.4 Progress towards increasing tertiary qualifications, 1998

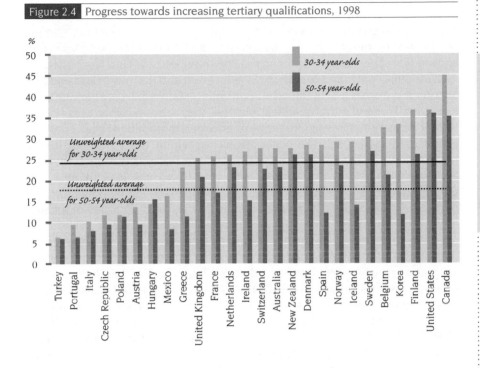

Countries are ranked in ascending order, by attainment level of 30-34 year-olds.

Source: OECD Labour Force Survey Database (2000).

Data for Figure 2.4, p. 145.

of 30-34 year-olds with tertiary qualifications lag the proportions found in leading countries and show either little evidence of catching up or, in a few cases, a widening gap.

For many countries, the higher attainment rates have occurred because of the expansion of tertiary education outside of university-based studies. In Austria, the Czech Republic, Denmark, and Finland – all countries with relatively low proportions of university graduates and little sign of change – alternatives to university studies are developing rapidly. Austria and Switzerland have introduced the *Fachhochschulen* and Finland established the AMK with the aim to attract young persons who otherwise would have followed university studies as their only viable option. The Finnish AMKs, from a very small base in the early 1990s, are expected to eventually account for more than two-thirds of all tertiary-level enrolment.

It seems safe to conclude that participation of young persons in tertiary education remains a long way from being universal. The consequences of less-than-universal participation at this level are more difficult to judge, depending in part on efficiency considerations, on each country's relative position, on whether adults can find their way into tertiary education and on whether "unmet demands" can be met outside the formal tertiary sector after individuals begin their careers.

... with many expanding capacity in advanced technical and vocational studies.

Lifelong learning seeks to facilitate upgrading of the competencies of poorly qualified adults, and updating of the knowledge of adults more generally.

3.4 Continuing education and training

Perhaps the single most important idea behind the concept of lifelong learning is that adults should continually update and, if necessary, upgrade their knowledge, skills, and competencies. The argument for this has rested on evidence that "once-and-for-all" initial education and training is less and less adequate as a basis for continued employability. Many adults are handicapped by the low levels of initial qualifications that they acquired when they left the formal education system. Others were adequately qualified when they left school, but have seen the occupations for which they prepared being transformed or disappearing altogether. There is solid evidence that, on average, better-educated adults earn more and are less likely to be unemployed. In this regard, completion of upper secondary appears to be particularly important.[2] It is claimed that the pace and skill-bias of techno-logical change make it increasingly important for adults to learn, whether by returning to formal education and training, participating in structured further education and training, or undertaking non-formal learning through on-the-job training, peer-coaching, or self-directed learning (Ernst & Young Center for Business Innovation and OECD, 1997; OECD and Statistics Canada, 2000; OECD, 2000c). It is argued as well that, in the "knowledge society", continual learning is needed to permit adults to stay active outside working life (OECD, 1996; OECD, 1997). How well equipped are OECD countries to address such needs? The discussion below approaches this question from two perspectives, one looks at institutional arrangements, the other at participation levels.

Institutional arrangements

But institutional arrangements are lacking…

Despite the widely held view that continuing education and training are important, there are only limited public institutional arrangements whose objective is to provide continuing education and training: adult education and labour market training programmes. Adult education typically comprises a small slice of total education provision under the auspices of ministries of education. On the education side, some of it takes the form of dedicated activities that aim to offer remedial education for adults with limited basic skills as well as other courses, vocational and non-vocational in nature, usually up through the equivalent of the secondary level. Some is in the form of incidental adult enrolment in initial formal education. Labour market training is provided through labour market authorities, usually to fill skill gaps for the unemployed or at-risk individuals. Moreover, proprietary/for-profit education and training providers typically provide courses that aim to raise competencies in relatively narrowly defined areas, such as foreign languages, computer and software skills, and certain business skills.

… and data for evaluating them, particularly for learning in non-formal settings are hard to come by.

Taking stock of institutional arrangements for adult education and training is difficult. Internationally comparable data exist on spending on and enrolment in labour market training programmes. But enrolment data are incomplete, and expenditure data for adult education and job-related training are limited. There are no enrolment or expenditure data on learning provided by

---

2. Evidence on this relationship has been presented in a wide range of OECD work including OECD (1994); OECD (1996); OECD (1997). For recent data on earnings and unemployment by educational attainment level, see OECD (2000a, pp. 270, 297-298).

proprietary/for-profit institutions, though some of that may be counted in enrolments in job-related training. These gaps in data make it difficult to evaluate the relative size of these different "sub-sectors", to say nothing of the extent to which they complement or substitute for each other.

What can be said about labour market training from a lifelong learning perspective? OECD countries spend on average about 0.2% of GDP on training mostly for unemployed adults and those at risk (OECD, 2000d, pp. 223-230, and Table 2.A in the Statistical Annex). The learning objectives are subordinate to the goal of placement in employment, and expenditures tend to be counter-cyclical (*ibid.*). Training for the unemployed typically is of short duration; enrolment sometimes is linked to eligibility for receipt of unemployment benefits (*op. cit.*, Chapter 4). In most countries, the place of such programmes in systemic approaches to lifelong learning is often weak and unintended.

However, in a number of OECD countries, labour market training programmes serve substantially more than the unemployed. In a third of the countries for which data are available, employed workers constitute nearly half of all the persons enrolled. In Belgium, Denmark, Portugal and Ireland, enrolments are sufficiently high to constitute an appreciable share of total enrolments in all adult education and training. In Portugal, for example, the number of employees newly-enrolled in labour market training programmes in 1998 equalled 9.3% of the total labour force. In that same year, an estimated 14% of adults participated in continuing education and training.[3] While this suggests considerable potential for the role of labour market training as a component of lifelong learning, there is as yet little basis to judge how well such programmes are integrated into a full range of learning options over adult life.

With a few exceptions, such as Portugal, countries do not appear to use active labour market policy as part of lifelong learning strategies.

To what extent is the formal education system accommodating the learning needs of adults? According to Figure 2.5 (next page), there are appreciable differences between countries. It shows that the share of total enrolments in formal education taken up by individuals 35 years of age and older, is under 4% of total enrolments in more than two-thirds of the countries for which data are available. This suggests that, for whatever reason, formal education either is not encouraging or is not facilitating participation by prime-age and older adults. But, the pattern is not universal. In Australia, the United Kingdom, Sweden, and New Zealand, 35-year-olds comprise 6% or more of total enrolments. Adult enrolments in formal education are concentrated in tertiary institutions. In several countries, tertiary education institutions are being urged to extend offerings to adults in degree as well as non-degree programmes. Although less common outside of such countries as Canada, New Zealand, the United Kingdom and the U.S., provision catering to adults now is seen both in terms of response to adult demand and, more pragmatically, as a means to maintain enrolments in the face of declines in the size of youth cohorts and secure revenues. Provision often takes the form of short programmes developed for industry and part-time and distance study options.[4]

Though formal education systems do not appear "adult-friendly", in Australia, New Zealand, Sweden, and the United Kingdom persons 35 years and older comprise 6% or more of enrolments ...

---

3. Detailed country data are provided in Tables 2.A and 2.B in the Statistical Annex.

4. This issue was addressed in a conference "Beyond the entrepreneurial university? Global challenges and institutional responses", organised by the OECD programme for Institutional Management of Higher Education in Paris on 11-13 September, 2000.

In all but a few countries, the adult share in secondary education is small. However, the adult share in tertiary education is greater, exceeding 10% in a large minority of countries.

| Figure 2.5 | Adult share in formal education by level, 1998 |

Percentage of adults aged 35 and over in enrolment

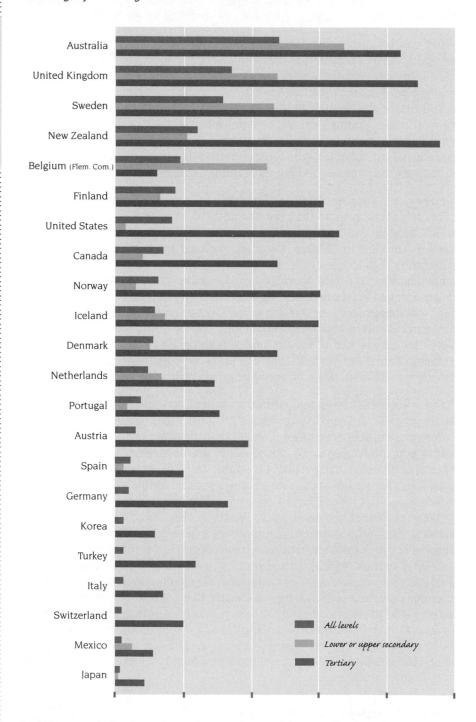

Countries are ranked in descending order, according to adult share of total enrolments.
Source: OECD Education Database.
Data for Figure 2.5, p. 146.

Although there is a recognised need for expansion of learning options below the tertiary level for adults with low educational attainment and literacy levels, the institutional responses have been limited. Persons 35 years old and older comprise more than 11% of secondary level enrolments in only four countries: Australia, the Flemish Community of Belgium, Sweden, and the United Kingdom. These patterns are linked in fairly obvious ways to policies and institutional arrangements deliberately geared to improving learning opportunities for adults. For example, in Australia, the technical and further education colleges (TAFE), and in United Kingdom, the further education institutions, endeavour to accommodate the needs of, among others, adults who have not completed secondary education. There are initiatives in other countries that are being put into place to redress the problem of limited opportunities for poorly qualified adults. In Norway, for example, authorities established in August 2000 the right for poorly qualified adults to complete secondary education as part of a larger package of reforms that also gives credit to individuals for non-formal learning. But the provision has not yet been implemented (details of how and where the needed education will be provided and financed are under negotiation), so it is too early to know how many adults will exercise the right to return to formal education.

... and in the Flemish Community of Belgium they comprise more than 11% of secondary enrolments.

Participation

A second way of taking stock of continuing education and training is to examine patterns of participation in learning activities, with the aim of quantifying how much individuals participate in learning activities regardless of the institutional setting. Although this approach does not shed light on how well public providers take care of adult learners, for example, it does provide some indication of the overall availability of opportunities for learners. There are a number of possible sources of comparative data on participation in continuing education and training (see OECD, 1999b, p. 140.) The International Adult Literacy Survey (IALS) is one of the most complete, with comparable detailed information from surveys of adults administered in 18 OECD countries. The survey collects information on participation in education and training (apart from on-the-job training) for the adult population.

Lifelong learning for adults also can be assessed in terms of participation in continuing education and training, and learning that occurs after completion of formal education.

On an analysis of survey responses, Figure 2.6 (next page) plots participation rates against the annual average number of hours of training received by participants. Participation rates and the average intensity (or duration) of training show little association.

Another way of assessing participation in further learning is to shift the focus from the learning process to outcomes, by considering how much adults learn once they leave the formal education system. In the absence of systems for assessing and recognising learning outcomes acquired during working life, it is necessary to construct proxy measures. Figure 2.7 does this for older adults, 46-65 years old, who completed upper secondary education some two to four decades earlier. It approximates "additional learning" that has occurred since completion of upper secondary education, by showing the proportion of that population who perform at or above the literacy level judged by experts to be above the literacy level that is typically associated with completion of upper secondary education. The larger the proportion that exceeds this minimum

The literacy levels achieved by older adults with upper secondary education vary among countries...

threshold, the greater the likelihood that adults are finding ways to acquire new skills and competencies. There are drawbacks to this approach. One is that the literacy measure captures just a slice of the spectrum of competencies that adults acquire over their working life. Second, it fails to control for differences in literacy levels that might have been observed when these adults first left upper secondary education. Third, this measure does not allow one to identify where and how adults learn. These caveats notwithstanding, this indicator does provide a crude measure of how much the undifferentiated combination of formal institutional arrangements, work-related training, on-the-job learning, and other factors contribute to adult learning.

... and appear to be linked to the extent of learning opportunities.

On this measure, as shown in Figure 2.7, large differences across countries may be observed. In the four countries with the highest values, adults with an upper secondary education are roughly four times as likely to have high literacy scores, as their counterparts in the three lowest ranking countries. The nature of initial education and training systems does not appear to be associated with differences in this proxy measure of learning outside of schooling. High and low-ranking countries include those with strong vocational tracks and those with a more general orientation in secondary education. On the other hand, differences in informal learning appear to bear some relation to opportunities for continuing education and training. The U.K., Sweden and New Zealand, which perform above average on this indicator, have relatively high rates of participation in continuing education and training. New Zealand and the U.K. also show relatively high levels of average annual hours of training for all adults (Figure 2.6).

Figure 2.6 | Adult participation in continuing education and training, 1994-98

Participation rates and average hours of training per participant

The rate of adult participation in continuing education and training is weakly associated with the duration of training.

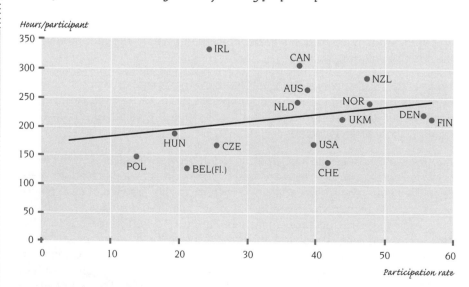

$y = 1.29 + 169.8, R^2 = 0.08$

Source: OECD and Statistics Canada (2000), *Literacy in the Information Age*, Table 3.11. ....
Data for Figure 2.6, p. 146.

| Figure 2.7 | Learning by older adults after formal education, 1994-98 |

Percentage of 46 to 65 year-olds with only upper secondary education performing at literacy level 3 or above (document scale)

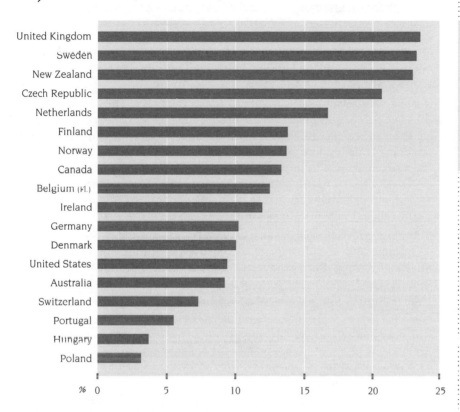

Countries are ranked in descending order.
Source: International Adult Literacy Survey Database.
Data for Figure 2.7, p 146

This section has reviewed evidence on what countries are doing to ensure sound foundations for lifelong learning and opportunities to pursue learning after initial education. Taken together, the set of indicators shows that in most countries the formal education sector is well-aligned with the objectives of lifelong learning in terms of achieving relatively high participation rates, especially in upper secondary education. The picture is much less satisfactory with regard to the new areas that the concept of lifelong learning attempts to embrace, namely learning demands in early childhood and adult life.

4. INCREASING THE AFFORDABILITY OF LIFELONG LEARNING

Implementation of lifelong learning for all poses complex resource challenges because it changes so many parameters at once. It implies potentially vast quantitative and qualitative changes in the content of learning and in where and when it occurs; changes in the costs of provision and total resource requirements; and shifts in financing burdens among various actors. The resource

Lifelong learning poses complex resource challenges because it changes so many parameters at once.

implications are highly dependent on institutional arrangements that range from school-building management, to entry barriers that deter private providers, to the tax treatment of training provided by employers. The resource implications also depend fundamentally on how ambitious a country is in its conception of lifelong learning and how ready public authorities and social partners are to engage in joint action. (OECD, 1999a; OECD, 2000e).

The affordability of lifelong learning depends on ...

However the resource implications are addressed, the underlying challenge is to find ways of making lifelong learning affordable. This depends on three broad strategies (see OECD, 1999a, pp. 24-25):

– raising the economic benefits of learning relative to its costs,

– *Raising the economic benefits of learning relative to its costs.* The "affordability" of lifelong learning depends on increasing the cost-effectiveness of learning in the various sectors in which it occurs – "increasing value for money". Insofar as this reduces costs (*e.g.* by making better use of facilities) and/or raises benefits (*e.g.* by improving the quality of learning outcomes), it raises internal rates of return to learning outcomes, thereby strengthening the economic incentives to invest in lifelong learning. This is essential for attracting net new resources for lifelong learning.

– allocating additional public resources in support of lifelong learning,

– *Allocating additional public resources in support of lifelong learning.* There may be an economic and social case for increasing the public spending effort on lifelong learning. Such resources may come in the form of net additional public spending or in the form of a reallocation from other areas of public expenditure to lifelong learning activities.

– reducing the cost of private investment in lifelong learning.

– *Reducing the cost of private investment in lifelong learning.* A substantial share of the burden for financing lifelong learning is likely to fall on employers and individuals and their families. This is because there appear to be substantial private returns to various forms of lifelong learning, particularly for tertiary education and continuing education and training. Also constraints on public spending and equity considerations make it unlikely that public authorities can pay all the costs. Increasing the private contribution is likely to depend on reducing the private cost of capital for such investment.

The discussion below examines evidence of country actions to carry out these broad strategies. It draws on some internationally comparable data, as well as on information collected under the OECD activity on finding alternative approaches to financing lifelong learning.

4.1 Strengthening incentives to invest in lifelong learning

Incentives to invest depend on lowering the marginal cost associated with increased enrolments.

If lifelong learning is to be affordable to societies, its economic benefits need to outweigh its economic costs enough to ensure that investments will pay for themselves (the cost of capital also plays a role; this is discussed later).[5] One factor that determines the affordability of lifelong learning is the direction

---

5. Economists approach this idea using "rates of return" to enable them to capture in a single term, economic benefits and costs, and the cost of capital. This approach has the advantage of permitting comparisons of different kinds of investment, using a single measure of economic efficiency. But the approach has methodological weaknesses that arise from the fact that rates of return are difficult to observe; they can only be observed ex-post. The approach being used in this subsection is to "unpack" rates of return into the components that drive economic benefits and costs, and the cost of capital. This is intended to shed light on the dynamic policy question of how to raise rates of return. For more discussion, see OECD (2000e); OECD (1998b, pp. 53-79); OECD (1998c, pp. 360-362); Wolter and Weber (1999); Wurzburg (1998).

that marginal costs take as the volume of learning activity expands. Will the per-student cost of additional enrolments in tertiary education, for example, go up as more students pursue studies at that level? If learning becomes more expensive as its total volume increases, it will be more difficult to generate substantial expansion of opportunities than if it gets progressively less expensive.

One crude approach to approximating marginal costs[6] is to see how per student costs vary with enrolment rates over time. There are limitations to this approach. First, it relies on budget data instead of costs. Insofar as outlays are a function of factors other than the underlying cost functions, such measures are misleading. However, it might be expected that changes in cost functions would work their way through the budgeting process. Second, the data on costs are highly aggregated, and so mask variations in configurations of classrooms, use of teachers and the use of technology. However, insofar as allocation decisions are made at an aggregate level, such an approach is relevant. Finally, these data are for formal education only; there are no comparable cost data for adult continuing education and training or for work-based learning.

Figure 2.8 shows trends in tertiary education, from 1990 to 1996. Only Australia and Spain experienced a relatively large increase in per student expenditure (exceeding 10%) in the face of moderate to substantial increases in enrolments. Increased enrolments were accommodated, in different measure in different countries, through flexible, less expensive arrangements (part-time and distance

In most countries marginal costs appear to be falling in tertiary education, and rising in schools, possibly as a result of measures to improve quality

---

| Figure 2.8 | Trends in expenditure per student and enrolment in tertiary education, 1990-96 |

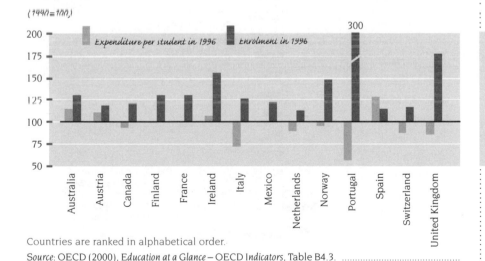

Tertiary enrolments increased everywhere between 1990 and 1996; in over two-thirds of the countries, these increases were associated with per-student costs that either remained steady or declined.

Countries are ranked in alphabetical order.

Source: OECD (2000), *Education at a Glance – OECD Indicators*, Table B4.3.

Data for Figure 2.8, p. 146.

---

6. It is virtually impossible to evaluate the marginal costs of expanded enrolment in formal education. Available data are aggregated at too high a level to capture costs at the level of the institution and to permit analysis of how costs vary with respect to increases in volume, and with respect to changes in the learning needs of the extra students who are served. It is even more difficult with respect to various forms of adult learning because the settings are too heterogeneous, and much of the cost is too complex to capture either in administrative or survey sources.

study options), channelling expansion into sub-sectors tertiary education with lower average per student costs, as well as through more intensive use of resources in conventional study programmes. By way of comparison, unit costs for primary and secondary education increased in real terms in the face of relatively stable or declining rolls in most countries for which trend data are available.[7] Countries that experienced the most substantial increases in per student expenditure (near or exceeding 15%) show different profiles. One group is comprised of countries where enrolment, in fact, has trended up (Australia and Austria). Another group is comprised of countries where modest declines in the number of students also coincide with measures to boost participation rates from a smaller school-age cohort and/or to raise the quality of education (Mexico, Norway, Portugal and Spain). Increases in expenditure per student when rolls are falling also may partly arise from difficulties in reducing committed spending on teachers and buildings in proportion to enrolment declines.

Education spending is increasing in most countries, particularly at the tertiary level. Growth in private spending, from small levels in some countries, has helped to finance expansion.

| Figure 2.9a | Trends in public and private expenditure on all levels of education, 1990-96 |

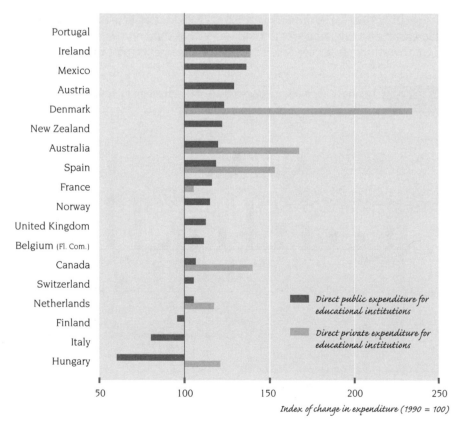

Index of change in expenditure (1990 = 100)

Countries are ranked in descending order according to change in public expenditure.
Source: OECD (2000), *Education at a Glance – OECD Indicators*, Table B1.2.

7. Detailed country data are provided in data for Figure 2.8 in the Statistical Annex.

4.2 Allocating more resources for lifelong learning

Earlier analyses by the Secretariat indicate that considerable financial resources would be required in most Member countries to implement the goal of lifelong learning for all. This is true even when the scenarios are restricted to ones of increased participation in formal education only (OECD, 1999*a*, Chapter 1; also see OECD, 1996, Chapter 8; and OECD, 2000*e*). Cost-cutting measures and measures to increase cost-effectiveness are intended to provide some room for manoeuvre in obtaining and extending the use of such resources. In some countries, demographic developments are expected to allow cost savings in line with falling enrolments. However, without reliable data on unit costs and particularly marginal costs, it is impossible to say whether the net new requirements can be met through either efficiency gains or savings from smaller student numbers.

Implementing lifelong learning goals requires considerable resources.

Public expenditure on education is a standard indicator of the availability of public resources for lifelong learning. Figure 2.9*a* shows that between 1990 and 1996 public expenditure for educational institutions grew substantially (near or exceeding 30%) in Austria, Ireland, Mexico and Portugal. To different

In most countries, public resources for learning are increasing in real terms.

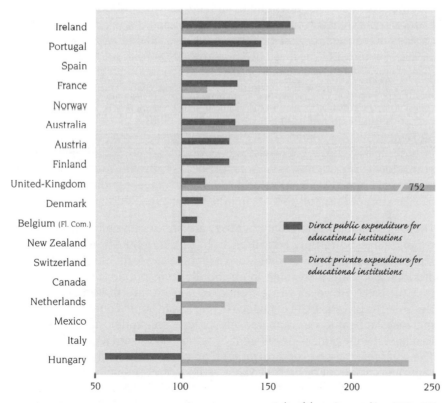

Figure 2.9b | Trends in public and private expenditure on tertiary education, 1990-96

Countries are ranked in descending order according to change in public expenditure.
Source: OECD (2000), *Education at a Glance – OECD Indicators*, Table B1.2. ....
Data for Figures 2.9a and 2.9b, p. 147.

degrees in these countries, the growth in public spending has accompanied school reforms aimed at boosting participation and/or increasing quality. Public spending declined in real terms in Finland, Hungary and Italy. In Hungary, fiscal consolidation in the early 1990s drove school spending down. At the level of tertiary education (see Figure 2.9*b*) Australia, France, Ireland, Norway and Spain increased public expenditure as part of the means to finance increased enrolment (see Figure 2.8).

Although public funds can be allocated in ways to encourage cost-effectiveness or improve equity, comparative evidence on such effects is lacking.

The allocation of public resources can be neutral with regard to its effects on incentives for efficiency or quality, such as those discussed in the preceding sub-section. Though targeted programmes such as labour market training for the unemployed aim to serve equity objectives, they can have the effect of favouring or excluding the *most* disadvantaged. In order to judge the impact of public spending on efficiency, quality and equity objectives advanced in the lifelong learning approach, it would be helpful consider *how* and *to whom* such resources are allocated. This could usefully complement the treatment of equity issues in Chapter 3. Unfortunately, detailed comparative data that would allow a comprehensive analysis on this issue do not exist. However, the available, limited data and some anecdotal evidence are suggestive.

These considerations come together in the financing of tertiary education. In a number of countries, the trend toward greater institutional autonomy has been accompanied by a growing interest in encouraging and enabling the choices of learners to influence the shape and quality of provision (OECD, 1998*a*). Funding approaches based on student enrolment and on subsidies directly provided to students work in this direction: under these approaches, tertiary education providers generate revenues partly on their ability to attract and retain students. Such approaches will have the most bite when supply can be brought on line to meet demand (particularly in high-demand fields) and where the public share of expenditure on tertiary educational institutions is high. In six OECD countries, the public share of spending on tertiary educational institutions was 90% or more in 1997. Overall, most public support is provided directly to institutions – 79% on average, ranging from less than 50% in Luxembourg to over 95% in Poland, Portugal, and Switzerland.

At the tertiary level there are signs of a shift in public resources away from institutions and towards students.

There is some indication that countries are shifting the allocation of public expenditures on tertiary education from tertiary education institutions to students. Public funds provided to students in the form of scholarships and student loans are increasing more rapidly than public funds provided to institutions.[8] However, these trends should be interpreted with caution. Because the private share of finance is very low in some countries, even small increases appear to be comparatively large. Also, student loans are subject to different arrangements in different countries, and so are reported differently. The sums refer to gross outlays rather than net spending (gross outlay minus repayment volume) or present-value estimates of the subsidy components of loans originated in a given year. Further, student support may be applied to living costs as well as to meet direct education-related expenses (*e.g.* tuition fees, books and supplies). Notwithstanding these considerations, the relatively more rapid growth in the volume of public spending for students implies a

8. Detailed country data are provided in Table 2.C in the Statistical Annex.

shift in financing strategies to support the choices of learners rather than to finance directly the supply of tertiary opportunities on offer.

Public investment in learning activities also occurs through labour market training programmes. As already noted, data suggest that public spending on such programmes declined, largely because of their strong counter-cyclical nature. Expenditure on adult labour market training declined in 12 of the 18 countries that experienced declines in unemployment in the late 1990s (OECD, 2000d).

Funding for active labour market programmes tends to be targeted on the unemployed...

Though there is no clear pattern with regard to labour market training for employed workers, Finland, Portugal and Spain stand out as interesting examples because labour market training appears to be somewhat more broadly consistent with a lifelong learning strategy. In each country, unemployment declined by nearly a quarter in the late 1990s. Labour market training expenditure for unemployed persons declined proportionately in Finland and Spain. During this period, both countries increased training for employed persons, in absolute terms as well as in the shares of labour market training expenditure. In Portugal, spending on training for employees also increased as part of a general increase in expenditure on labour market training. However, an examination of overall patterns and trends in expenditure data for labour market training for adults seems to show that resource allocation decisions have *not* taken place with lifelong learning strategies in mind. There is probably limited potential value in doing so, given the counter-cyclical nature of such programmes. That said, the patterns observed in Finland, Portugal and Spain suggest that, insofar as policy permits training for employed workers, it is worth investigating further the possibility that such resources might be deployed as part of larger strategies for lifelong learning.

... but in Finland, Portugal and Spain, funding appears to be available to employed workers.

4.3 Reducing the cost of capital for private sector investment in lifelong learning

Decisions to invest in lifelong learning are influenced by numerous factors. The preceding sub-section takes stock of how *public* funds are channelled for investments in lifelong learning. This sub-section considers how *private* financing is being encouraged and channelled.

Education through the secondary level is commonly viewed as a public good, and the public sector bears financial responsibility for it.[9] This is not the case for tertiary-level studies or for continuing education and training for adults. At the tertiary level, private contributions are substantial in some countries (over 50% in Japan, Korea and the United States), and the private share of expenditure on tertiary education institutions is growing almost everywhere. Indeed, the most striking feature of trends over the 1990s displayed in Figure 2.9*b* is the growth in *private* expenditure on tertiary education (though as already mentioned, the increases have been from very low bases in some countries). Except in France and Ireland, private expenditure on education increased more rapidly (if from a smaller base) than public expenditure. The role of private financing differs among groups of countries. Australia, Ireland and Spain are countries where expanding enrolments were

Though public resources are increasing in tertiary education, the private share is increasing more in most countries.

9. This does not preclude private provision of elementary and secondary education, or private finance of some share of such privately provided education.

financed through relatively large increases in both public and private expenditure. Canada, Hungary and the Netherlands are countries where relatively stable or declining (Hungary) public expenditure was accompanied by substantial increases in private expenditure. In the United Kingdom, growth was financed through a moderate increase in public expenditure and a substantial increase in private expenditure. Developments to the end of the 1990s reveal a dynamic, changing picture: Portugal's largely fee-supported private universities and polytechnic institutes account for about one-fourth of overall tertiary education enrolment and so imply substantial private expenditure on learning at this level; the continued growth in revenues generated through deferred payment of contributions in Australia now accompany roughly steady public expenditure; and tuition fees in conventional tertiary education in Hungary and Ireland have been eliminated.

Expansion of financial resources for adult education and training is likely to be from the private side.

In the financing of adult education and training, private sources account for the largest share (90% by Secretariat estimates). For this sector, public policy and framework conditions assume critical roles in generating needed resources through, among other means, reducing the cost of capital.

The cost of capital is an important consideration because individuals and companies are shouldering an increasing share of investments in learning.

The affordability of private investment in learning activities depends on the economic benefits relative to the economic costs (for an individual, this might be the increase in wages that come with acquiring a new skill, and the cost of tuition and foregone earnings associated with training, for example). It also depends on the cost of capital, that is the interest charges on the capital sum necessary to finance the investment. Charges incurred on a bank loan used to finance the investment are explicit. The charges may be implicit, taking the form of forgone interest on the amounts withdrawn from a savings account to finance the investment.

It has been argued that lifelong learning investments are handicapped because the cost of capital for such investments is higher than the cost of capital for more traditional forms of investment. For individuals, this is so because loans used to finance the investment have higher interest charges than loans for buying a house or other durables. Insofar as such investments are financed out of savings, they are paid for with after-tax income. For companies, the higher costs take the form of lower market valuation (lower share price) because, unlike other forms of investment, there are no means for reporting or otherwise signalling in a credible manner to the stock market the return from such investments. They also can take the form of higher interest charges on loans to cover such investments, insofar as the capital or expected value of the "assets" acquired – skills and competencies – is not captured in conventional financial accounting and reporting practices[10] (see Ernst & Young and OECD, 1997; Mortensen, 1999;[11] Ministry of Economic Affairs, the Netherlands, 1999; Blair *et al.*, 2000).

---

10. Experts cite market valuations of companies that have nothing to do with company profitability or other "fundamentals", as evidence that conventional financial accounting and reporting practices fail to capture the most important sources of value creation in the "knowledge economy". See Blair *et al.* (2000); Levitt (1999).

11. For more details on the international proceedings on measuring and reporting intellectual capital, see http://www.oecd.org/dsti/sti/industry/indcomp/act/Ams-conf/symposium.htm.

The issue of the cost of capital for investment in lifelong learning is a relatively new area for public policy. There are no indicators to assess comparative progress in this area.

Options for reducing the cost of capital still are at an exploratory stage.

In taking stock of how lifelong learning is financed, there is evidence of both progress and gaps. On the one hand, expenditures are following trends in participation in some countries; where they are not, somewhat higher unit costs may be a consequence of reforms as well as of fixed arrangements for the deployment of staff or buildings. Moreover, there is considerable evidence of piecemeal strategies that could lead to increases in the volume of resources available to finance expanding participation in lifelong learning and to improvements in cost-effectiveness, rationalised public spending and reduced cost of capital for investment. On the other hand, little progress has been made in placing the financing of learning in each sector within a system-wide approach to the allocation and use of resources for lifelong learning. The assessment of progress in these areas awaits further experience in countries having recently adopted new financing approaches as described in Chapter 1, and the development of new measures to monitor performance in this area.

Progress towards making lifelong learning an affordable investment has been piecemeal – comparative assessment is not practical.

5. ATTEMPTING A SYSTEMIC ASSESSMENT OF LIFELONG LEARNING

It is difficult to draw general conclusions about where countries stand in implementing a mandate that is both broad and open-ended because they differ with respect to starting points and relative priorities. Differences in country-specific circumstances and needs imply that countries will want to go in different directions, and therefore pursue different objectives. Moreover, few countries have established objectives against which one could evaluate progress towards the implementation of strategies for lifelong learning (OECD, 2000e).

Though it is not possible for a single indicator to capture overall performance …

The preceding sections have attempted to address some of these difficulties by drawing on the best available internationally comparable data to calculate indicators that provide some measure of how countries perform with respect to particular elements in a lifelong learning strategy. But we still lack measuring rods against which to judge country progress at a systemic level, across all the relevant dimensions of lifelong learning, *i.e.* indicators against which to judge overall progress in meeting the goal of lifelong learning for all. That being the case, we have to fall back on more qualitative judgements based on the evidence presented in the preceding sections.

… the preceding indicators do suggest certain general conclusions …

1. The Nordic countries stand out with *good performance* across *multiple sectors*, though each appears to miss at least some of the essential building blocks that comprise *systems* of lifelong learning. Each has weaknesses, particularly with regard to participation in ECEC, completion of upper secondary education, and/or adult learning. Most have strong results for inputs, such as completion of upper secondary education; all come out well on measures of quality of schooling, completion of tertiary education, and participation in continuing education and training. Performance is uneven with respect to literacy levels among older adults, possibly because popular adult education sometimes is separate from activities that address the learning outcomes measured by IALS. Although it might be argued that cultural homogeneity

… the Nordic countries have good performance across multiple sectors, though each appears to miss at least some of the essential building blocks …

makes it easier to achieve such balance, all these countries have substantial foreign populations and have responded to increases in immigration with programmes explicitly aimed to facilitate social integration.

... Canada, the Czech Republic, Germany, the Netherlands, and New Zealand also do well, but have gaps in more areas ...

2. A second tier of countries – Canada, the Czech Republic, Germany, the Netherlands, and New Zealand – also do well, but have certain gaps or weaknesses in more areas. Canada and New Zealand perform relatively less well in term of literacy levels among adults; the Netherlands do well on literacy scores but has offsetting weaknesses in learning opportunities for adults.

... Australia, Switzerland, the United Kingdom, and the United States are uneven in their performance ...

3. A third tier, including Australia, Switzerland, the United Kingdom, and the United States, is characterised by comparatively weak and uneven performance on the available measures. In Australia, the United Kingdom, and the United States, adults are well represented in formal education systems, but do less well on measures of literacy. Switzerland has high rates of upper secondary completion, but low rates of learning by adults beyond formal education, and low participation in ECEC.

... Ireland, Hungary, Portugal and Poland appear to do poorly in comparison to other countries; still all are undergoing substantial reforms in initial education.

4. Finally, a fourth tier of countries – Ireland, Hungary, Portugal, and Poland – do poorly in comparison to other countries on most measures. By history and circumstances, older persons in these countries are, on average, less qualified than elsewhere. All have implemented sweeping and ambitious reforms, the effects of which have yet to be released. In all these countries, there has been a high priority given to improving education opportunities for the young. Judged by past patterns, they perform well; judged in comparison to countries against which they compete in global markets, there is an evident need to persist with and strengthen these efforts.

With respect to lifelong learning value for money...

Lifelong learning, like any other public policy, is not something to be pursued at any cost. Its implementation has to compete with other priorities for scarce public resources. This raises the question of how countries compare with respect to the *cost-effectiveness* of their strategies for lifelong learning: how they compare in getting the most value for money spent on lifelong learning? One way to evaluate this is to consider whether the groupings of countries discussed above bear any relationship to the amount spent on formal education systems.

... the Nordic countries spend more on learning than anyone else, but they appear to get results. For most other countries the picture is mixed.

In fact, the picture is mixed. The countries in the first tier stand out as the biggest spenders by a wide margin. In Denmark, Finland, Norway and Sweden, direct public expenditure for educational institutions (the usual measure of public spending education) averaged 6.6% of GDP in 1997, 1.5 percentage points more than the average for the other countries. They spend more and they get more, at least with regard to the measures included in the stocktaking. Moreover, the real differences in cost-effectiveness may be greater, because other countries rely to a greater extent on additional private-source finding. For other countries the picture is less clear: there is little or no association between the rough assessment of their relative performance and their public spending effort on education.

When one scans the indicators covering the diverse components of lifelong learning, the overall picture that emerges raises two issues. The first, on a substantive level, has implications for the formulation and implementation of lifelong learning policy. The stocktaking exercise suggests that only a minority of countries seem to be well on the way to making lifelong learning for all a reality. In the majority of countries, lifelong learning is largely an unfinished agenda. For the few that are consistently low relative to other countries on various indicators considered here, one might ask whether lifelong learning should be a high priority, in view of the pressing needs to consolidate initial education, schools in particular. For most of the rest, the stocktaking suggests that, though countries may fully subscribe to the goal of making lifelong learning for all a reality, they vary in their capacity to formulate and execute strategies for achieving such a goal. The shortcomings raise questions that range from the most obvious – is a country investing adequate financial resources – to more complex, such as whether opportunities are accessible on an equitable basis, how quality is assured, and whether diverse policies are mutually supportive in achieving systemic change. These questions bear further investigation.

In sum, only a minority of countries seem to be well on the way to making lifelong learning for all a reality.

The second issue, a technical one, is whether the picture that emerges from the various indicators is real, or the product of mis-specification of goals and objectives, and/or mis-measurement of inputs and outcomes. As was pointed out at the beginning, the stocktaking is drawing on existing data, rather than data that were collected for the express purpose of taking stock of lifelong learning. Some of the individual indicators that are considered in the preceding sections are crude approximations and merit further technical refinements. The stocktaking exercise also would benefit from less heavy reliance on the International Adult Literacy Survey and greater flexibility in the choice of indicators to reflect better the fact that countries differ with respect to their specific objectives and strategies for implementing lifelong learning. Whatever proxy measures are chosen, it is essential to have time-series data so as to capture evidence of change over time. But in view of the fact that so much of lifelong learning is built on existing learning arrangements that are fairly well documented, the technical weaknesses mentioned here probably would not alter the overall picture very much. After all, the overall picture is consistent with the view that emerges from other sources of information, such as the OECD education policy reviews and thematic reviews.

Although indicators constructed from the best available data may have technical limitations, the overall picture is consistent with the view that emerges from other sources of information.

Certainly the overall view should be sharpened, and possibly quantified so as to make it easier for policy makers to better understand and manage lifelong learning at a *systemic level*. At this point it would appear that such a composite measure of the systemic performance of national systems of lifelong learning might lack credibility, in view of the technical shortcomings outlined above, and the political sensitivity of the implications of what such a composite might reveal. It is for precisely such reasons that more definitive systemic indicators are needed. Without them, debate over legitimate differences in political preferences and strategies, become clouded by a lack of transparency in the underlying facts.

Presently a composite measure of systemic performance would lack credibility, but such a measure is needed.

6. CONCLUSIONS

This chapter represents a first attempt to take stock in a systematic way of where countries stand with respect to the realisation of lifelong learning. Individual country performance has been examined with respect to two broad lifelong learning goals: *a*) coverage and outcomes in foundation and

This chapter represents a first attempt to take stock of the implementation of lifelong learning.

continuing learning; and *b*) how resources are being marshalled and used to make lifelong learning affordable. A wide range of comparative information on participation, completion, literacy and financing has been brought together in an effort to produce a set of comparable and meaningful indicators for a large number of OECD countries.

Ad hoc indicators have been constructed for doing this, though they are not ideal measures.

Such an exercise is essential to the process of further translating the concept of lifelong learning for all into operational objectives, and, in the longer term, for evaluating progress towards realising those objectives. This exercise presently strains against the limits of the available information base, partly because lifelong learning as an orientation for policy and practice remains at early stages of definition as well as implementation in many countries. Data either are not fully comparable or are lacking on several key dimensions of lifelong learning. The assessment of where countries stand on the realisation of lifelong learning is forced to rely on *ad hoc* indicators constructed from existing data on inputs and outcomes of existing programmes and arrangements. The absence of time-series data for many of these proxy measures makes it impossible to evaluate progress over time, or to capture the effects of recent policy initiatives. These difficulties are compounded when one tries to establish internationally comparable indicators on new as well as conventional aspects of performance because there are important differences among countries in inputs and context, as well as fundamental approaches to lifelong learning. So, the indicators presented in this chapter provide only a partial assessment of where countries stand on the realisation of lifelong learning.

One can conclude that countries differ considerably in the extent to which they have the ingredients for systems of lifelong learning ...

Notwithstanding the difficulties, the comparative stocktaking of lifelong learning presented in this chapter has value because it gives weight to learning at *all* stages and to a wide variety of forms of learning. In comparing countries on the basis of the indicators considered in this chapter, a number of conclusions are particularly noteworthy:

– There is considerable variation across countries with regard to the extent that they have achieved balance among the different sectors in which lifelong learning occurs. A few countries – notably the Nordic countries, Canada, the Czech Republic, Germany, the Netherlands and New Zealand – show up well consistently on the various indicators used in the chapter. They show balance across sectors. Those that do less well are countries in which there is less balance, due to high priority being placed on raising educational attainment levels, or insufficient attention given to ensuring quality of schooling outcomes, for example.

– For other countries it would appear that further progress is needed with respect to participation in and/or outcomes of formal education systems. But it is important to add that the formal education system is not the only platform for further progress. At the level of early childhood education and care, some of the Nordic countries, Australia and the Netherlands opt for policies to favour early childhood development in the home. Further out on the lifelong learning spectrum, Belgium, Portugal, Spain and to a lesser extent, Ireland enrol appreciable numbers of adults – employed as well as unemployed – in labour market training programmes, thus showing a readiness to supplement whatever employers and individuals might be doing.

– There are encouraging signs that Member countries are addressing the resource and financing issues that arise as they implement policies for lifelong learning. On the basis of the indicators considered in this chapter, it would appear that efficiency in the formal education sector is rising in many countries. This will reduce the financial constraints on further expansion. Constraints on the expansion of tertiary education are being eased by the rising contributions of students and their families. Although there are no indicators regarding resources and financing of adult learning, several countries have recently put in place innovative measures to reduce the private cost of capital of such investment.

A number of other conclusions also can be drawn from this chapter. One is that policy makers are "flying blind" when it comes to lifelong learning. Although there are sound, empirically-based arguments for policies that favour lifelong learning, there still is a scarcity of information on how much progress countries have made in realising lifelong learning, and on what works and what does not. It is virtually impossible to measure how well different areas of policy work together as systems of lifelong learning. Without such feedback, it is impossible to manage progress towards achieving the goals of lifelong learning.

... but when it comes to knowing what they have accomplished, policy makers are flying blind in many respects.

A second conclusion is that there are critical gaps in internationally comparable information in two areas. One concerns the costs of learning and, in particular, the extra costs associated with expanding provision in various settings, both inside and outside the formal education sector. The second concerns the volume and nature of learning activity and outcomes outside the formal education sector. Notwithstanding the considerable progress achieved through INES and IALS, there remain large gaps that must be closed if policy makers are to make informed decisions.

There are critical gaps in internationally comparable information, particularly regarding costs of learning and the volume and nature of learning in non-formal settings.

A third conclusion is that it seems feasible to develop and refine internationally comparable indicators for taking stock of progress towards realising lifelong learning, including measures to assess overall performance. To be sure, such indicators are approximations; inevitably they reflect biases as to the goals and objectives of lifelong learning. But, importantly, they provide a measuring stick for comparing countries. OECD will play its part, together with Member countries and other international organisations and the European Commission in seeking to develop and refine such indicators and use them to improve policy making. ∎

It seems feasible to develop and refine internationally comparable indicators for taking stock of progress towards realising lifelong learning.

References

BLAIR, M. and **WALLMAN, S.** (eds.) (2000), *Unseen Wealth: Report of the Brookings Task Force on Understanding Intangible Sources of Value*, The Brookings Institution, Washington, D.C.

BRADBURY, B. and **JÄNTTI, M.** (1999), "Child Poverty across Industrialized Nations", UNICEF International Child Development Centre, Innocenti Occasional Papers, Economic and Social Policy Series No. 71, Florence.

ERNST & YOUNG CENTER FOR BUSINESS INNOVATION and **OECD** (1997), *Enterprise Value in the Knowledge Economy: Measuring performance in the age of intangibles*, Cambridge, MA.

EUROPEAN COMMISSION (2000), *Key Data on Education in Europe*, Luxembourg.

LEVITT, A. (1999), "Quality Information: The Lifeblood of Our Markets", Remarks of the Chairman of the U.S. Securities & Exchange Commission to the Economic Club of New York, New York City, October 18.

MORTENSEN, J. (1999), Programme Notes and Background, prepared for "Measuring and Reporting Intellectual Capital: experience issues and prospects – An International Symposium", organised by the OECD, Netherlands Ministry of Economic Affairs, Netherlands Ministry of Education, Culture, and Science; Nordisk Industrifond, Amsterdam, 9-11 June.

NETHERLANDS MINISTRY OF ECONOMIC AFFAIRS (1999), *Intangible Assets: Balancing accounts with knowledge*, The Hague.

OECD (1986), *Girls and Women in Education: A cross-national study of sex inequalities in upbringing and in schools and colleges*, Paris.

OECD (1994), *The OECD Jobs Study: Evidence and Explanations*, Paris.

OECD (1996), *Lifelong Learning for All*, Paris.

OECD (1997), "Lifelong Learning for Employability", document, Paris.

OECD (1998a), *Redefining Tertiary Education*, Paris.

OECD (1998b), *Human Capital Investment: An International Comparison*, CERI, Paris.

OECD (1998c), *Education at a Glance: OECD Indicators*, CERI, Paris.

OECD (1999a), *Education Policy Analysis*, CERI, Paris.

OECD (1999b), *Employment Outlook*, Paris.

OECD (2000a), *Education at a Glance: OECD Indicators*, CERI, Paris.

OECD (2000b), *From Initial Education to Working Life: Making Transitions Work*, CERI, Paris.

OECD (2000c), *Knowledge Management in the Learning Society*, CERI, Paris.

OECD (2000d), *Employment Outlook*, Paris.

OECD (2000e), *Where are the Resources for Lifelong Learning?*, Paris.

OECD and **STATISTICS CANADA** (2000), *Literacy in the Information Age: Final report of the International Adult Literacy Survey*, Paris.

U.S. DEPARTMENT OF EDUCATION and **OECD** (1999), *How Adults Learn*, Proceedings of a conference held April 6-8, 1998, Georgetown University Conference Centre, Washington, D.C.

WOLTER, S.C. and **WEBER, B.A.** (1999), "Skilling the unskilled – a question of incentives?", *International Journal of Manpower*, Vol. 20, No. 3-4, pp. 254-269.

WURZBURG, G. (1998), "Issues in financing vocational education and training in the European Union", *Vocational Training*, No. 13, January-April, pp. 22-26.

CLOSING THE GAP: SECURING BENEFITS FOR ALL FROM EDUCATION AND TRAINING

SUMMARY

In knowledge economies, the distribution of education and lifelong learning has profound effects on social equity. Broad access to learning could narrow inequalities, but the opposite will happen if human capital becomes concentrated – the more so because it can be passed from one generation to the next.

Disappointingly, in recent decades of educational expansion, the educational outcomes of more privileged and less privileged groups have not converged markedly. Children from poor or less educated families, from ethnic minorities and with disabilities remain well behind. The story for women is better: they are now being educated to the same levels, on average, as men, although still being paid less.

Such inequalities are today compounded by inferior access among traditionally disadvantaged groups to computers and the Internet, especially at home. However, more even access to such technology in schools has helped counter this inequality. Policies to tackle the digital divide need to be integrated into general policies to combat disadvantage.

Finally, inequalities can be further compounded in adulthood because adults tend to engage in more education and training if they are already well educated. However, some countries have been relatively good at spreading participation more evenly.

Overall, educational equity has proven highly elusive. With the stakes higher than ever, the chapter ends with a list of priorities for strengthening commitment to this goal.

1. INTRODUCTION

As globalised, knowledge-oriented societies prosper, they see the risk of growing inequalities ...

A critical challenge for emerging knowledge-based societies is to build and maintain social cohesion. At the heart of political debate and action is a growing awareness that global changes promising to enhance overall prosperity also risk increasing inequalities and dividing societies. This could increase the polarisation that has already taken place in many countries recently. For example, an OECD study of 21 countries found that income inequality grew in more than half of them from the mid-1980s to the mid-1990s, with simultaneous rises in the proportion of households that are "work-rich" and the proportion that are "work-poor".[1]

... and would like to promote equitable access to human capital. This chapter interprets educational equity in the new context of the knowledge economy ...

The central importance of the distribution of human capital makes the role of education and training more crucial than ever in pursuing social equity and cohesion. Politicians and social commentators have long recognised the potential for education to contribute to greater equality, but have also acknowledged that it can sustain and accentuate social division. Equity is now an entrenched value in most public education systems, and is likely to continue to be so. But this chapter takes a fresh look at what this means for the ways in which learning is structured at the beginning of the 21st century. The chapter reviews a series of new challenges in fostering educational equity, such as the importance of learning throughout life and the need to avoid a "digital divide". In these circumstances, achieving equity goals requires more than just ensuring wider access to learning for disadvantaged groups; it also requires that the kinds of learning most needed in the knowledge economy be delivered to them.

... looking respectively at evolving priorities, at who has gained from educational expansion, at the digital divide and at equitable access to lifelong learning.

Section 2 gives a short overview of the ways in which educational equity is important in the 21st century. Section 3 looks at the recent trends and the degree to which particular groups have shared the expansion of education attainment. Even though average overall educational levels have increased greatly over the past few decades in almost all countries as demonstrated in Chapter 2 of this publication, the relative position of the disadvantaged has not always improved. Closing these gaps requires not just greater participation of excluded groups to higher levels of education than in the past, but also ensuring that they avail themselves of the new forms of learning which are needed. Sections 4 and 5 review learning trends in this changing context, first with respect to the digital divide and the specific requirement of using technology effectively, and then more generally in terms of the need for lifelong learning. The concluding section highlights some policy initiatives within education and training that can contribute to more equity in education and learning, thereby helping to foster greater social cohesion.

2. NEW AND OLD REASONS TO CARE ABOUT EDUCATIONAL EQUITY

Who accesses learning matters a lot to our societies ...

The distribution of education and learning in any country is a matter of profound political, social and economic importance. An abundant literature[2]

---

1. See Förster (2000) for details.
2. Reviewed, for example, in OECD (1994, 1998b).

shows that investment in education and training is beneficial for individuals and for enterprises. Adults with higher educational attainment have, on average: better employment and pay prospects, better health and life expectancy and less chance of being involved in crime. Enterprise-based training can produce gains to individuals in terms of higher wages and better careers and to firms in higher productivity and profits.

A key political issue is therefore how access to, and the benefits from, education and training can be made available to as many people as possible, including those with disabilities, members of low socio-economic groups, ethnic minorities and others facing disadvantages. Educational inequalities in this respect have tended to reflect social inequalities more generally, but governments today aim to make their systems more inclusive. The Department for Education and Employment in England, for example, aims "to give everyone the chance, through education, training and work, to realise their full potential, and thus build an inclusive and fair society and a competitive economy".

... so efforts to extend access are politically important ...

While the desire for education to promote social justice dates at least from the advent of universal schooling a century ago, some recent trends have brought new urgency to this ambition:

... the more so in light of the economic importance of human capital, the profusion of ICTs, the risk to families and communities from weakening social bonds and the importance of a good initial education to support lifelong learning.

— The growing importance of *human capital* in knowledge-oriented societies has already been mentioned. New jobs will continue to be concentrated in high-skilled services, although OECD economies will continue to generate many low-productivity jobs, especially in social and personal services. This may create new skill-based inequalities within the labour market and/or exacerbate existing ones.

— The use of *information and communication technologies* (ICTs) is expanding rapidly in OECD countries. This has given rise to much debate about the emergence of a "digital divide", with negative consequences for equity goals (see Section 4 in this chapter).

— A weakening of traditional *social bonds* creates further imperatives for education and for schools. In the case of families, for example, the past three decades have seen higher rates of family break-up and growth in the number of lone-parent families. Such families are at high risk of social exclusion. In such a context, the school's importance grows as an institution that can bring communities together, while schooling itself has a key role to play as an experience to which every child has access. Schools can also play a valuable role in building community networks and social capital, especially where traditional support structures have weakened.

— There is a growing recognition that *lifelong learning* is important for success in a constantly changing world. Since active learning in adulthood has always tended to be concentrated among those with a better initial education, greater pursuit of lifelong learning has the potential to lead to even greater social polarisation based on access to knowledge.

3. HOW WIDELY HAS PROGRESS IN EDUCATIONAL ATTAINMENT BEEN SHARED AMONG DIFFERENT GROUPS?

The persistent minority not completing secondary education risks being marginalized ...

As Chapter 2 shows, access to upper secondary and tertiary education has grown dramatically in all OECD countries over the past three decades, yet a minority of varying sizes in different countries continues to be at risk due to low educational attainment. As shown in Section 5 below, these inequalities can be accentuated in adult life, as opportunities for further learning are often greater for the most highly educated. So a significant fraction of the population in many OECD countries is in a marginal situation in relation to learning and employment opportunities.

... with certain groups being particularly at risk.

How well have groups that traditionally did poorly in education fared in this context? This section reviews the situation of four such groups that have figured prominently in the debate in all countries: people of low socio-economic status; women; ethnic and other minority groups; and people with disabilities. These are not the only groups subject to "a marginal position" within education – for example members of rural and isolated communities are clearly disadvantaged in some countries. Relevant equity categories may well shift over time as targets for some groups are achieved, as new categories become relevant (for example, women have in general caught up with men in terms of educational attainment (although some countries are doing better than others). Finally, it is not uncommon for individuals to exhibit several of these characteristics at the same time, compounding disadvantage.

3.1. Equity and socio-economic background

First, how have students from lower-income and less-educated families fared recently?

Have students from low-income families improved their access to tertiary education over time compared with students from high-income families? Does better education still pass down largely through families, from one well-educated generation to the next? Is the access to prestigious universities still mainly reserved to high professional and income groups?

Young adults with less-educated parents inherit low human capital more strongly in some countries than others ...

There is little comparative material across OECD countries on the relationship between educational output and socio-economic background. The International Adult Literacy Survey has, however, compared the literacy scores achieved by young adults (16-25 years old) and the length of their parents' education in years. In all countries, people with better educated parents are more literate, but the strength of this relationship varies considerably across participating countries. In the Nordic countries, for example, the literacy scores for young adults are relatively high and vary less with parental education than in the other countries, suggesting that these countries have been relatively successful in combating inequalities in educational outcomes among young people.

... but a French study shows that socio-economic background remains the strongest factor associated with educational differences ...

In France, 62% of the 15-year-olds (9th grade) coming from the poorest 20% of the families have had to repeat at least one year in school compared with 17% of the 9th graders from the richest 20% of the families. The study also shows that, even if there are many factors behind this significant difference in young peoples' performance, the socio-economic background is the strongest factor of explanation (INSEE, 2000).

Box 3.1 Socio-economic background and access
to tertiary education

- In **Australia**, the share of students with a low socio-economic background in tertiary education has fallen slightly over the period 1991-97. They represent 25%[3] of the population but only 14.5% of higher education students in 1997 as compared with 15% in 1991 (Department of Education, Training and Youth Affairs, Australia, 1999).

- In **France**, the socio-professional category of the parents has a strong influence on the study their children undertake. Students whose father is a *cadre supérieur* or *professeur* have approximately 17 times more chances to be in a *classe préparatoire*[4] and five times more to study at university (*1er cycle*) than the children of a worker. There seems to be little change in this pattern over time: students whose father had a tertiary education constituted 31 and 35% of the university population in 1982-83 and 1996-97, respectively. The equivalent figures for students whose fathers are workers, are 12.6 and 12.7%. Although there is a greater part of the French population who has a tertiary education and a smaller part that are workers in 1996-97 compared with 1982-83, there seems to be little progress over time for low socio-economic groups in their access to tertiary education (Attali, 1998).

- In **Germany**, the majority of 17-18 year-olds come from a low socio-economic background (52%). Out of 100 pupils belonging to this group only 33 succeed in transferring to the *Gymnasiale Oberstufe* (upper secondary grades of the *Gymnasium*). For those from a high socio-economic background the corresponding figure is 84%. Only eight out of a hundred young people with a low socio-economic background succeed in gaining access to higher education. For a young person from a high socio-economic background, the probability of making the transition is 72%. In the old German Länder, 14% of higher education students are from the group with a low socio-economic background. In 1982, the corresponding figure was 23%. The percentage of higher education students from the group with the highest socio-economic background has risen, from 17% in 1982 to 29% in 1997, in the old Länder. There are marked differences between the Länder in terms of students' socio-economic background.

- In **Ireland**, less than 25% from the two social groups "Unskilled Manual Workers" and "Semi-Skilled Manual Workers" went to higher education in 1998 compared with over 75% from the three social groups "Farmers", "Employers and Managers", and "Higher Professionals". The highest proportionate increase has however, occurred for those social groups which had very low participation rates in 1980 (HEA, 2000*b*).

- In the **United Kingdom**, a recent survey by the Sutton Trust showed that the chances of being enrolled in one of the top 13 English universities are about 25 times greater if the student attended an independent (private) school than if he/she came from a lower social class or lived in a poor area. In addition, children from less affluent social classes represent 50% of the school population, but only 13% of entrants to top universities (Sutton Trust, 2000).

---

3. People from low socio-economic status backgrounds are defined as those whose postcodes of permanent home addresses fall within the lowest 25% of the population of a given region, determined by the Australian Bureau of Statistics Index of Education and Occupation.

4. A *classe préparatoire* is the prestigious preparation for the entry examinations to the *Grandes Écoles* in France.

- In the **United States**, the percentage of high-school completers aged 16-24 who were enrolled in college the October after completing high school varied considerably with family income throughout the period 1972-96 (see Figure 3.1).[5] Even though the students from families with a low income have improved their access to college over the period 1972-96, there remains an important social gap: 46.8% of students from low-income families, 62.7 from middle-income and 78% from high-income families enrolled in college in 1996. However, compared with 1972 the gap between students' access to college has somewhat narrowed between the three family income categories (NCES, 2000c). However, to receive a college degree, a student must have successfully reached three milestones: high-school graduation, college participation and college completion. Over the past two decades, there has been little change in high-school graduation rates at each quartile of family income (Post-secondary Education Opportunity, 1998). Furthermore, over the past two decades, among the lowest quartile of family income college completion declined, while at the highest quartile it increased. The end result is that over the past two decades there has been a growing inequality in college completion between the lowest and highest quartiles of family income.

5. The low-income families are defined as those families with the bottom 20% of all family incomes; the high-income families are the top 20% of all family incomes; and the middle-income families are those with the 60% income in between.

Figure 3.1 College entrance by family income, United States, 1972-96

Percentage of high-school completers aged 16-24 who were enrolled in college the October after completing high school

Americans with a high-school degree from low-income families are twice as likely to enter college now than a generation ago, but remain far less likely to do so than their wealthier peers.

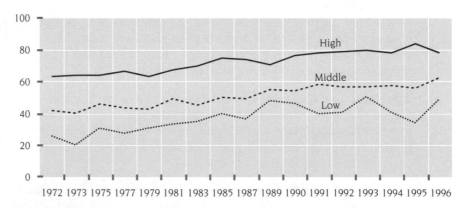

Source: NCES – National Centre for Education Statistics (2000), "Quick Tables and Figures".
Data for Figure 3.1, p. 148.

... and various studies show no closing of the gap between different social groups ...

The French example is not unique. The examples from other countries cited in Box 3.1 show that, despite a high political awareness that lower socio-economic groups often do not have equal access to tertiary education compared with higher socio-economic groups, there is little or no long-term progress in narrowing this social gap. The situation has not improved over the past decade. Analysis in OECD (1999*d*) finds that enrolment rates in the 1990s have often recorded below-average growth among lower socio-economic groups, and concludes:

> "The expansion has not on the whole reduced disparities in access to tertiary education for people from different backgrounds: the extra places have been taken up at least as much by children from more privileged socio-economic groups as by others. Countries that wish to improve such access are therefore having to make conscious and sustained efforts to help prepare and assist all students rather than assuming that the creation of more places will be sufficient" (p. 65).

The issue of under-representation in tertiary education of children from low socio-economic status families remains high on the equity agenda. However, the issue is not as straightforward as it might seem. It would be a mistake to assume that the category "low socio-economic status" is static. Note that the long-term effect of general educational expansion is to increase the size of better-educated groups across successive generations. Nevertheless, expansion and diversification have not made a great impact on the relative chances of the worst-off, even in those countries that have striven hard to create more equal learning opportunities for all.

... with expansion of tertiary education not reducing inequalities in access to it: an enlarged group of better-educated families retains its relative advantage.

3.2. Equity and gender

The proportionate rise in educational attainment at both upper-secondary and tertiary levels has in every OECD country been greater for women than for men over the past three decades. This has been a case of catching up. Among those currently aged 55-64, only 6% of women compared with 12% of men have university degrees or equivalent, and 38% of women compared with 50% of men have upper secondary completion. For 25-34 year olds, the genders are, on average across OECD countries, exactly equal in attainment levels: 16% of both men and women have university-level and 72% upper secondary qualifications.

Second, women have now caught up with men in educational attainment on average ...

Indeed, women's average educational attainment now exceeds that of their male counterparts in a number of OECD countries. The ratio of upper secondary graduates to total population in 1998 was more than 10 percentage points higher for women than men in Canada, Finland, Greece, Ireland, Portugal and Spain; the same is the case for net entry rates in "type A" tertiary education[6] for Australia, Finland, Iceland, Ireland, New Zealand, Norway, Spain, and Sweden. In contrast, the ratio of upper secondary graduates to total population is 10 percentage points higher for men than for women in Austria, Switzerland and Turkey and the same is the case for the net entry rates in tertiary-type A education in the Czech Republic, Japan, Korea and Turkey (OECD, 2000*a*).

... with young women getting higher qualifications in some countries, and men in others ...

While female enrolment rates in tertiary education have risen sharply, significant gender differences continue to exist, however, in the programmes studied at university, with women more likely to enrol in fields related to the health professions, education and the social and behavioural sciences, and

... but gender differences persist in terms of what is studied, and men are more likely to do PhDs ...

---

6. Tertiary-type A programmes (ISCED 5A) are largely theory-based and are designed to provide sufficient qualifications for entry to advanced research programmes and to professions with high skill requirements.

less in the natural sciences and industrial and engineering fields. While there has been an increase in the enrolment of women in first-degree tertiary education programmes in sciences, engineering and business, in most countries considerable imbalances remain. Women are also under-represented in Ph.D. programmes (HEA, 2000*a*).

... which could help explain continuing pay gaps between equally well educated men and women.

These differences in study patterns may contribute to the fact that women continue to earn less on average than men, regardless of their educational level. Figure 3.2 compares women's to men's earnings at similar levels of education by age group. For all OECD countries, women's annual earnings are much lower than men's, irrespective of their educational attainment and age. This overall picture illustrates how, despite significant progress in women's access to learning opportunities, they are still far from achieving equality in earnings. However:

This gap varies by country;

- The **size of earnings inequalities** varies greatly across countries. Women in the age group 30-44 years *without upper-secondary* education in Finland, Hungary, Denmark, Portugal and Sweden earn most relative to men – between 71% and 77% of what men earn. In comparison, women in the same age group with similarly low credentials in the United Kingdom, the Netherlands, Canada, New Zealand and the United States earn only around 50% of the salaries of less-educated men. In the case of women with *tertiary education* in the age group 30-44 years, in Ireland they come closest to men's salaries with over 90%, and in Portugal, Denmark, Spain and Finland they are between 71 and 76%. At the other extreme in Italy, the Netherlands, New Zealand and the United States, they earn only between 57% and 66%.

... in some it is wider and in others narrower for better-educated groups;

- The **effect of more education** on earnings equalities does not follow a consistent pattern. In the Netherlands, New Zealand and the United Kingdom, the differential narrows considerably with increasing educational attainment. In a number of countries, by contrast, including Italy and Sweden, the reverse relationship tends to be true: earnings differences between men and women tend to be particular high at the tertiary level. Thus, although higher educational attainment is generally associated with higher earnings for both men and women, it does not seem to contribute systematically to reductions in gender inequalities (OECD, 2000*a*).

... varying career patterns helps explain differences;

- Different **career and occupational choices** can explain some of the differences between men and women's earnings, as can differences in the amount of time men and women spend in the labour market, and the relatively high incidence of part-time work among women.[7]

... as do family patterns;

- The fact that women earn less than men also reflects that most people for most of their working lives are in **families with multiple incomes** and that women often are working less when the children are young.

---

7. This is *e.g.* the case in the Netherlands.

| Figure 3.2 | The relative earnings of women in successive generations |

Mean annual earnings of women as a percentage of men's earnings at the same educational level, ages 30-44 and 55-64, 1998

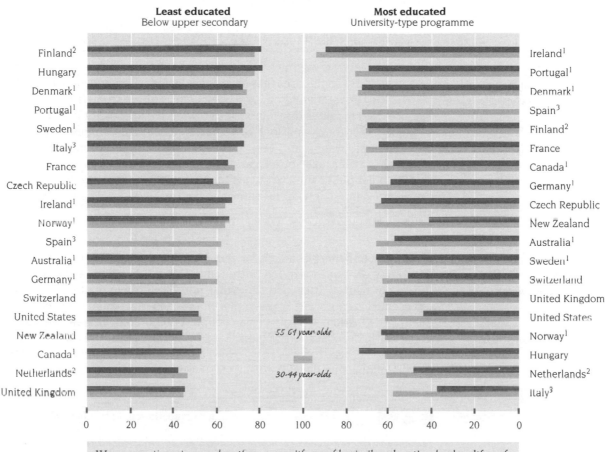

Women continue to earn less than men with roughly similar education levels, although the gap is narrower for younger adults in most countries.

1. 1997.
2. 1996.
3. 1995.

Countries are ranked in descending order by mean annual earnings of women as a percentage of men's earnings.

Source: OECD (2000), *Education at a Glance – OECD Indicators*, Table E5.2.

Data for Figure 3.2, p. 148.

— Figure 3.2 shows at least some ***movement towards more equality of earning*** between one generation and the next. Although the movement is not dramatic, in most countries gender disparities are lower for the younger age group shown. This is especially the case for women with a tertiary educational background. The change has been greatest in the four countries in which older women graduates earn below half their male peers: Italy, the Netherlands, New Zealand and the United States.

… and in some countries poorly-paid women graduates are starting to catch up.

*Third, ethnic minorities, i.e.
migrants, indigenous groups
and "historically
disadvantaged"...*

*... are being targeted to
combat often multiple
disadvantages ...*

*... but some, though not all
such groups continue to do
badly – so even sharper
targeting is needed.*

3.3. Equity and minority groups

Three main groups are distinguished as ethnic minority groups in this chapter because they are often targeted as such in equity educational programmes:

1. Migrant groups in societies;
2. Minority indigenous populations;
3. "Historically disadvantaged"(*e.g.* African Americans, Gypsies, etc.).

Historically, minority groups have often not had equal access to learning resources and in some cases they have been denied basic human rights. Today, many OECD governments have taken specific policy initiatives to counterbalance the difficulties that minorities are meeting in education both related to the fact that they might not have mastered the main language taught in the education system and their different cultural backgrounds. However, specific initiatives taken by educational authorities have often to be followed up with other public initiatives to address compound disadvantages arising from, for example, low socio-economic background combined with a poor urban or rural location.

Despite these efforts, the examples mentioned in Box 3.2 show a pattern of continuous under-achievement for certain ethnic groups which starts in early education, continues through further and higher education, and persists in the labour market. They also show that not all ethnic minorities are underrepresented in education. For example, Indians and some other Asian people in the United Kingdom and some Asian people in the United States are in general doing well in the education system and in the labour market. This indicates that equity policies need to focus sharply on disadvantaged minority groups and the conditions affecting their access and achievements in education.

| Figure 3.3 | College entrance by racial or ethnic group, United States, 1972-96 |

Percentage of high-school completers aged 16-24 who were enrolled in college the October after completing high school

In the United States, the college entrance rate for white high-school completers has risen more than for Black and Hispanic students.

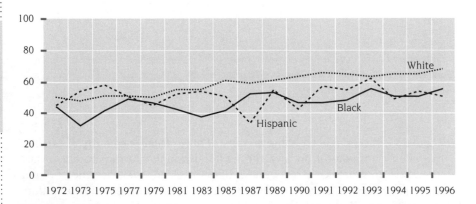

Source: NCES – National Centre for Education Statistics (2000), "Quick Tables and Figures". ....
Data for Figure 3.3, p. 149.

Box 3.2 Access of ethnic minorities to education

- In **Australia**, the Indigenous Australians have achieved an equitable representation among students entering tertiary education. However, nearly 20% of Indigenous Australian entrants in 1997 was enrolled in enabling courses, compared with only 1% of non-Indigenous Australians. Furthermore, the apparent retention rate of Indigenous students is only 78% that of non-Indigenous students (Department of Education, Training and Youth Affairs, Australia, 1999).

- In the **United Kingdom**, Bangladeshi, Black and Pakistani origin pupils perform less well than other pupils in the early key stages of education. Pupils from these three ethnic groups also tend to achieve significantly less by the end of compulsory education. Educational under-achievement is even more acute for Gypsy and Traveller children, only a small minority of whom remain in education to age 16. A youth cohort study of 18-year-olds in England and Wales shows that, at the age of 18, a higher proportion of Indians and whites has a level 2 equivalent qualification or higher (83 and 68%, respectively) than Black (48%) or Pakistani/Bangladeshi students (56%) (DfEE, 2000).

- In the **United States**, the percentages of high-school completers aged 16-24 who were enrolled in college the October after completing high school were respectively 67, 56 and 51 for White, Black and Hispanic students in 1996. As shown in Figure 3.3, the rate at which this entry rate increased between 1972 and 1996 was particularly high for white students (up 17 percentage points) and less for the black students (up 11 points) and the Hispanic students (up 6 points). Furthermore, the percentage of 18 through 24-year-olds who completed high school shows that both Blacks (81%) and Hispanics (63%) are below the average for the American 18-24 year-old population (85%) (NCES, 2000c).

3.4. Equity and people with disabilities

In numerous OECD countries a particular effort has been made to integrate people with a disability into the regular system at all levels of education. Issues of equity and civil rights have been important determinants in this development, but other influences include changes in parents' attitudes, teacher supply and training, better equipped schools, and the introduction of ICTs (OECD, 1999e). Students with a disability distinguish themselves from other equity groups in the sense that disability can affect individuals from families throughout the social structure, and randomly at any time.

Fourth, various efforts have been made to promote equity for people with disabilities ...

It is estimated that 15 to 20% of students will, at some stage of their school career, call upon services relating to special educational needs. OECD work on statistics and indicators on special education (disabilities, learning and behaviour difficulties, and disadvantage) shows that there is a wide range of different understandings in OECD countries on how to define special educational needs. Some countries, for example, recognise only students with traditionally-defined physical or severe mental disabilities, while others include learning difficulty and disadvantage.

... which can vary with the many ways that countries define special educational needs.

*Although more such
students' participate in the
mainstream of education,
their success in accessing
more advanced levels of
study has been mixed.*

Despite the efforts that have been made to improve access and achievements of students with disabilities at the different educational levels, the examples in Box 3.3 show that they are still under-represented in education. OECD work shows that the situation is poor for disabled students in the transition phase between compulsory and non-compulsory education and equivalently qualified disabled students have a harder time on the labour market (OECD, 1997c). Nevertheless, the past decades have shown considerably higher participation and achievements of disabled students from primary to post-secondary education in many countries. The equity challenge in education for this group has now been transformed in most countries to one of providing an inclusive approach within an accessible environment.

4. THE DIGITAL LEARNING DIVIDE

*People unable to use ICTs
fall further behind in a
knowledge-oriented society ...*

It is often argued that the increasing use of ICTs is giving rise to new inequalities in access to learning and work opportunities. Those without access to ICTs and without ICT skills become less and less capable of participating in the knowledge-based society, which makes increasing use of technology and information. The resulting so-called *digital divide* represents a major challenge for policy-makers at all levels.

Box 3.3 Equity and people with disabilities

- In **Australia**, despite an increase in participation in tertiary education (2.4% of tertiary students identified themselves as having a disability in 1997 versus 1.8% in 1996), the disabled population is still under-represented (4% of the relevant population group have disabilities). However, the retention rate for students with a disability is almost identical to the rate for other students (Department of Education, Training and Youth Affairs, Australia, 1999).

- In **Germany,** the proportion of students with a disability is about 2% (15th Social Survey of Student Life). Students with a disability or chronic illness, however, more frequently change discipline, degree or higher education institution. Among those whose studies have been strongly impaired by health difficulties, there is an above-average rate of change of higher education institution (25%) and of study interruption (34%) (Schnitzer *et al.*, 1999).

- In the **United Kingdom**, according to the Labour Force Survey, about 7% of the 18-30 age group reported a longstanding disability, while only 4% of higher education students did. Furthermore, 18% of the 18-year-olds with a disability or health problem had at least achieved a level 3 qualification, while 39% of the 18-year-olds without a disability or health problem had obtained such a qualification (DfEE, 1999).

- In the **United States**, according to a NCES report on students with disabilities in post-secondary education, 63% of such students were enrolled in post-secondary education two years after completing high school by 1994 versus about 72% for students without disabilities. The students with a disability were more likely to choose a shorter post-secondary education than those without. In a cohort of students who had earned bachelor's degrees in 1992-93, 4% of those without disabilities, and 11% with disabilities, were unemployed in April 1994 (NCES, 1999).

One can distinguish between at least three dimensions of the "digital divide": *a*) differential access to computers and the Internet by socio-economic background, ethnic group, age, and educational background; *b*) geographic differences (between cities, regions, countries); and *c*) variation in ICT use by type of company (small *vs* large; different sectors).

Figure 3.4 presents the percentage of households possessing a personal computer (PC) and the ratio of students per computer in upper secondary education for various OECD countries in 1998. As shown in the top half of Figure 3.4, the percentage of households with a computer varies from a high of 63% in Denmark to a low of 20% in Italy. The bottom half of the figure shows that the number of upper secondary students per computer ranges

... a disadvantage that can arise from lack of access, geography or type of company.

Access varies greatly across countries, but computers are not always plentiful in schools in the same countries where they are plentiful in homes ...

Both at home and at school, students' access to computers varies widely in different OECD countries.

Figure 3.4 | Home and school access to computers in OECD countries, 1998

A. Percentage of households possessing a PC

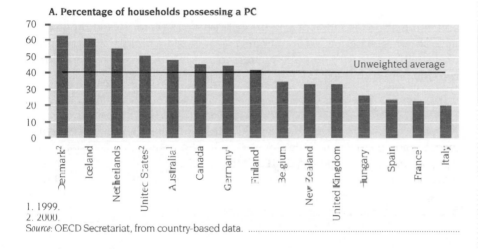

1. 1999.
2. 2000.
Source: OECD Secretariat, from country-based data.

B. Students per computer in upper secondary education

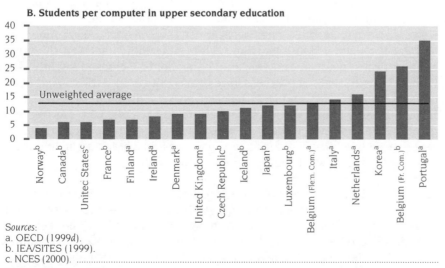

Sources:
a. OECD (1999*d*).
b. IEA/SITES (1999).
c. NCES (2000).

Data for Figure 3.4, p. 149.

from 4 in Norway to 35 in Portugal. So, although investment in hardware, software and telecommunication links in families and educational institutions has been growing fast in all OECD countries, resources remain unevenly distributed across OECD countries. Moreover, Figure 3.4 reveals that there is not a positive correlation in some countries between coverage of PCs in homes and coverage of computers in upper secondary schools. Countries like France and the United Kingdom have a below-average student-computer ratio (relative high coverage) in upper secondary education, and a below-average coverage of PC's in homes. For the Netherlands, the opposite is the case.

... and awareness of the educational value of ICTs is leading educators to look for alternative out-of-school access for those without computers at home.

Schools and education authorities are well aware of the importance of integrating ICTs into teaching and learning, both to prepare students for the information society and to make the most of new learning tools. Policy-makers are encouraging schools, libraries and learning centres to invest in computers and access to the Internet in order to reduce the disadvantage of those who have no access to ICTs in their homes, by enabling them to access learning and information resources at a public institution. Data from the United States have shown that people without home computers are almost 1.5 times more likely than people with home computers to get outside access to the Internet through public libraries or community centres (NTIA, 1999).

4.1. Do the digital divides increase existing inequalities?

Home ICT access is linked with social and, in some countries, geographical advantage ...

A key concern with respect to the digital divides is whether they reinforce existing income and wealth inequalities. Country studies from Australia, Canada, France, Italy, Sweden, Turkey and the United States all show that access to computers and the Internet is very dependent on socio-economic, ethnical and educational background. In some countries (Australia, Canada and Italy), differential rates of access by geographic location are a serious issue.

... for example minority groups in the United States have fallen behind, but could now start catching up ...

Data from the United States and the United Kingdom confirm this pattern. Between December 1998 and August 2000, there has been a surge in uptake of Internet and computer access among all households in the United States. However, the gap in access rates between, on the one hand, Asian-American and Pacific Islander households and White households and, on the other hand, African-American and Hispanic households increased slightly (see Figure 3.5). In 1998, the access rates for White and African-American households were 29.8% and 11.2% respectively, or a "divide"of 18.6%. By 2000, the comparable figures on access rates were 46.1% and 23.5%, leading to a gap of 22.6%. However, if the more rapid rates of growth in Internet access experienced by African-American and Hispanic households are maintained, this "digital divide" will begin to narrow (NTIA, 2000).

... while in the United Kingdom almost none of the poorest 40% of households are online, but as costs come down, some of these inequalities could reduce.

Figure 3.6 shows home access to the Internet by gross income decile group in 1998-99 and 1999-2000 in the United Kingdom. As few as 3% of poorer households are online, compared with 48% of more affluent households. This disadvantage is severe throughout the poorest 40% of the population, well under 10% of whom are currently on-line. Nevertheless, as in the US case for some minority ethnic groups, the poorest households have experienced a higher growth in expansion rates from 1998-99 to 1999-2000 than the wealthiest households in the UK. So, the poorest households, those with low educational background and some ethnic groups are at the present being left behind in the digital revolution. The observed differences between groups in rates of access to the Internet may partly be accounted for by costs (relative to income) and partly by literacy levels (Human Resources Development Canada, 2000). As improvements are realised in these areas, rapid increases in rates of usage among previously low-use groups might be maintained.

Figure 3.5 Percentage of U.S. households with Internet access by racial or ethnic group, 1998 and 2000

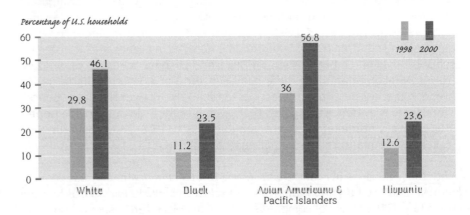

Sources: NTIA (1999), *Falling through the Net: Defining the Digital Divide.*

Some minority and low income groups continue to lag in Internet access.

Figure 3.6 Home access to the Internet by gross income decile group in the UK, 1998-1999 and 1999-2000

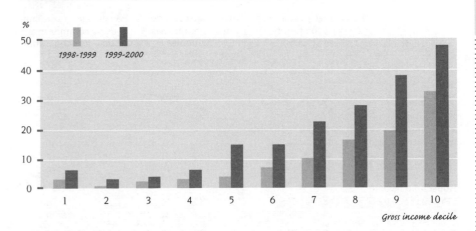

Source: National Statistics, UK (2000), *Internet Access.*
Data for Figures 3.5 and 3.6, p. 149.

*A growth of school students
using computers for
schoolwork…*

*… shows far less home
usage for poorer and ethnic
minority groups, but similar
amounts of school usage …*

*… while growing usage at
work has particularly
affected better educated
workers, with less variation
by race or ethnic group.*

4.2. Access to ICTs in schools and in the labour market

Table 3.1 shows the percentage of 1st to 8th grade students using computers at school, at home, and at home for schoolwork by gender, ethnicity, and household income in the United States in 1993 and 1997. In the period from 1993 to 1997, there has been an increase in the 1st to 8th graders who use computers at school, and especially in the percentage of students who use computers at home and at home for schoolwork.

There is almost no difference in 1997 between how many girls and boys use computers at these ages, although these data do not show how much time is spent using them. Furthermore, there is only a minor variation in the use of computers at school between different ethnic and socio-economic groups, with White children and those from higher-income families using computers slightly more often than children from other backgrounds. The gap has narrowed over the period 1993-97. In contrast, use of computers by white children and children from higher-income families in homes and at home for schoolwork is much higher than for Black and Hispanic children or children from low-income families. There has been little or no narrowing in use at home, either for personal interests or for schoolwork over the same period. Thus, there is evidence to suggest that, even if schools do not provide poorer students and ethnic groups with equal access to ICTs, they generally help lessen the inequality in access that exists at home (OECD, 1999d; NTIA, 1999).

With the high use of ICTs at the work place, low technology literacy has come to represent in itself an important form of exclusion in societies. As can be seen from Table 3.2, the use of computers at the work place varies significantly with the level of income and education and less so with race/ethnicity and sex in the United States. Over the period 1993 to 1997, there have been few changes in the overall picture of who uses computers at work. The overall percentage of workers

Table 3.1 **Student use of computer in 1st-8th grades in the United States, 1993-97**

	Percentage of students using computers at school		Percentage of students using computers at home		Percentage of students using computers at home for schoolwork	
	1993	1997	1993	1997	1993	1997
Sex						
Male	70	80	25	44	10	24
Female	68	79	25	43	12	24
Race/Ethnicity						
White, non-Hispanic	74	84	31	54	14	30
Black, non-Hispanic	57	72	9	21	4	10
Hispanic	58	68	8	19	3	10
Household income						
$15 000 to $19 999	68	75	11	16	5	8
$75 000 or more	79	86	62	81	29	49
Total	**69**	**79**	**25**	**43**	**11**	**24**

Source: NCES (2000), *Digest of Education Statistics 1999*.

Table 3.2 **Percentage of workers, 18-years-old and over, using computers on the job, 1993 and 1997 in the United States**

	1993	1997	Increase in percentage points
Sex			
Male	40	44	4
Female	52	56	4
Race/Ethnicity			
White, non-Hispanic	49	54	5
Black, non-Hispanic	36	40	4
Hispanic	29	30	1
Family income			
Less than $20 000	25	27	2
$75 000 or more	66	70	4
Educational attainment			
Not high school graduate	10	12	2
Master's degree	71	79	8
Total	**46**	**50**	**4**

Source: NCES (2000), *Digest of Education Statistics 1999.* ....

using a computer at work has only risen slightly from 46 to 50% over the period. However, a UK study found more dramatic growth: in 1999, 60% of workers used computers in their jobs, up from an estimated 24% in 1992 (Wright, 2000).

Several OECD countries, *e.g.* Australia, Canada, France and the United States have targeted programmes to bridge dimensions of the digital divide. The divide is rooted in broader societal and economic issues. It is therefore necessary to address a wide range of policy initiatives to bridge the divide such as education, skill development and training, as well as telecommunication issues such as pricing of equipment and access costs. Some OECD countries have launched programmes, among others, for: children and schools in poor neighbourhoods, providing extra financial help for ICT investment;[8] ICT training of low-skilled workers; tax initiatives for companies to encourage private investments in ICT training; donation to community technology centres, etc. Many countries are devoting greater attention to improving the ICT skills of teachers (OECD, 1999*d*).

Efforts to address this divide have had to tackle wider social inequalities.

5. EQUITY AND LIFELONG LEARNING

When considering how to reduce levels of social and economic exclusion due to shortfalls in adult skills and competencies, policy makers need to address more than just inequalities in educational attainment and access. It is now well understood that to be of greatest use on the labour market and in society more widely, people need to learn in ways that can be put to practical use throughout life. Above all, they need a set of general competencies that

Today, educational equity should mean giving people the skills to go on learning, not just access to initial education ...

8. For example, the E-rate initiative in the United States, in which schools and libraries benefit from 20 to 90% discount on telecommunication services, shows that the poorest schools (greater than 50% of students eligible for free and reduced-cost lunches) represent only 25% of public school students but receive 60% of the funds.

equip them to go on learning and adapting to new contexts. This is not identical to being able to complete courses and pass exams in initial periods of education and training.

... so low levels of basic adult skills such as literacy are disturbing.

The International Adult Literacy Survey (developed jointly by the OECD and Statistics Canada) aims to measure directly the ability of adults to complete tasks using written materials in the kinds of situations encountered in everyday life and at work. In 14 out of the 20 countries that participated in the survey, at least 15% of all adults aged 16-65 performed at literacy level 1 – a level which expert opinion judges to be too low to cope with the most basic tasks required in a knowledge-based society. These countries are: Australia, Belgium (Flanders), Canada, Chile, Czech Republic, Hungary, Ireland, New Zealand, Poland, Portugal, Slovenia, Switzerland, the United Kingdom and the United States. The survey data show, furthermore, that there are significantly fewer opportunities to work for adults with low literacy skills: they are less likely than average to be in employment, less likely to find work when looking for it, and less likely to work regularly when a job is obtained. For example, in Australia, Belgium (Flanders), Canada, Denmark, Germany, Ireland, Finland, New Zealand, Slovenia and the United Kingdom, the incidence of unemployment is twice as high among adults with low literacy skills than among adults with medium to high skills.

Better literacy profiles among younger adults may indicate better educational outcomes, but also skills could be deteriorating during adulthood ...

The survey shows that young adults aged between 26 and 35 have higher literacy scores than adults aged 56-65 in every OECD country participating in the survey. This can partly be explained by the fact that the younger population in OECD countries is more likely to have received extended formal education. However, this is not the whole explanation as the survey also indicates that, even when only adults with completed secondary education are included, the skill differences by age remain. This could possibly reflect a positive trend in the quality of education over time, but is also likely to be affected by the experiences undergone in adulthood.

... which strengthens the case for continuing education and training – which unfortunately tends to be concentrated among the already well-educated ...

One important influence on the development of competencies during adulthood is access to further education and training. Training rates vary by level of initial education. This arises, in part, from behaviour by employers which government programmes have limited scope to counteract. Employers spend much more resources on training their high-skilled, well-educated employees than their low-skilled, low-educated employees. The proportion of individuals receiving financial support from the public sector for training is less than 10% in 16 of the 20 countries which participated in the International Adult Literacy Survey. Even after controlling for full or part-time work, firm size and occupational category, those workers in Canada, Chile, the United Kingdom and the United States who make greatest use of their literacy skills at work are six to eight times more likely to receive support from their employers for education and training than those who use workplace literacy skills the least (OECD and Statistics Canada, 2000).

... although differences in participation can be greater between countries than between the best- and worst-educated group in one country ...

In general, then, training of adults tends to reinforce skill differences resulting from unequal participation in schooling in OECD countries. But this difference is much greater in some countries than in others. Figure 3.7 shows, for example, that the participation rate of the least educated adults in the United Kingdom and New Zealand in education and training is greater than that of university graduates in several other countries. For those who do engage in training, its intensity varies, but in no systematic fashion: in Ireland, for example, people with low education who participate do so for relatively large amounts of time; in Canada and Poland, it is the most qualified whose training is of greatest duration.

Other evidence indicates that training is most evenly distributed across educational levels in Ireland, Japan, New Zealand, the Netherlands and several Nordic countries, and least equally in Belgium, Hungary and southern Europe (OECD, 1999c). Training rates also decline with age, but this also varies greatly across countries. Workers aged 50-54 years receive almost as much training as those aged 25-29 in the United States and the Nordic countries (except Finland), while the older group receives much less training than the younger in France, Greece, Portugal and Spain. So progress in reaching the goal of lifelong learning for adult workers has been uneven.

... and some countries succeed in reducing this tendency of the already-educated to engage in most adult learning.

Figure 3.7 Participation in job-related education and training by employed adults with different educational levels, 1994-95

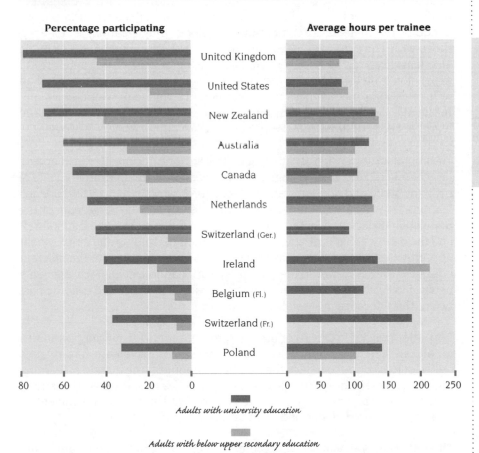

Percentage participating   **Average hours per trainee**

United Kingdom
United States
New Zealand
Australia
Canada
Netherlands
Switzerland (Ger.)
Ireland
Belgium (Fl.)
Switzerland (Fr.)
Poland

80   60   40   20   0   0   50   100 150 200 250

Adults with university education

Adults with below upper secondary education

In all countries, those with more education participate more in training. However, there is less of an association between educational attainment and the duration of time spent in training.

Source: OECD (2000), *Education at a Glance – OECD Indicators,* Table C7.4.
Data for Figure 3.7, p. 149.

6. CONCLUSIONS

Exclusion of some groups from learning has a heavy cost.

Knowledge-based economies and societies cannot afford to exclude a large part of their population from access to education and learning resources. Furthermore, inequalities in society often raise problems of mutual understanding and adjustment within organisations, in society at large and in the democratic process.

The problem must be tackled on a wider field than just education ...

The issues of equity are broadly social, cultural and economic and not just educational. There are cultural and social norms at stake, political interests and active pressure groups at work. Education policies alone will not be sufficient in addressing the equity challenge. Clearly, social inequalities existing outside the education system contribute to educational inequalities in terms of access, opportunity, process and outcomes as well as in terms of the consequences of achievements and attainment.

... while educational policies themselves need to have equity priorities built in.

All OECD countries are pursuing equity goals through education policies. What is less certain is the extent to which other guiding policy aims within education (*e.g.* improving accountability or the promotion of market mechanisms in education) have supported or counterbalanced the pursuit of equity. The challenge of combating exclusion through learning is not easy: those with acute learning needs are most at risk of exclusion, while being also least likely, as we have seen, to become lifelong learners. Therefore, an expansion of lifelong learning may in itself potentially exacerbate rather than reduce existing inequalities. To counterbalance this, equity strategies and initiatives in lifelong learning must ensure that barriers to learning and learning needs of those most at risk are addressed.

The failure to narrow gaps in access and attainment at a time of great expansion must be worrying ...

The impressive expansion of participation in education documented in Chapter 2 has contributed to a steady progress in the average educational attainments of the populations and work forces in OECD countries, which in general has widened learning opportunities. There is, however, still a relatively large part of the population, especially people from low-income families, some ethnic minorities, and the disabled that is disadvantaged in relation to learning and employment opportunities. For some there has been improvement in access to the different education levels. However, the gap in educational access and achievements between different economic and ethnic groups has not narrowed over the past two to three decades in several OECD countries.

... so we should acknowledge this policy failure, even though solutions are not easy ...

Education policies in OECD countries to promote equal learning opportunities for all can therefore hardly be seen as successful. Gaps remain, and there is still a lot to be done to reduce the number of people at the margin of learning and employment opportunities. There are no easy solutions: the equity challenge is real, and prior policy responses have not proven sufficient to address what are dynamic and complex learning needs for all.

... and set the following objectives in the future:

The following policy initiatives to promote greater equity in education and learning are not intended to be exhaustive, but aim to give guidance to governments on what kinds of education and learning initiatives can combat social exclusion. They are based on intensive OECD work on education and equity (OECD, 1997a, 1997c, 1998a, 1999b, 1999e, 2000g) and the evidence from this chapter:

– **Aim for good-quality upper-secondary education for all.** Educational attainment both at secondary and perhaps even more at tertiary level is likely to continue growing over the coming years. In particular, countries where a significant minority of young people still does not complete upper-secondary will want to move towards universal completion. The focus should, however, not only be put on a quantitative perspective, where participation is counted in terms of mere attendance, but also on a qualitative imperative where such access and participation will fall short without good-quality teaching and genuine learning. Obtaining basic skills in literacy and numeracy for all is, for example, an important "quality" goal for education systems.

– **Adapt to individual needs.** The education system (especially upper secondary and tertiary education) should be diversified, flexible and open to good practices (including, for example, adoption of new forms of teaching and learning), in order to be able to include students who are less skilled academically. Diversification and flexibility can, for example, be provided by distance learning and by recognition of work experience (informal learning) as part of the study programmes. Norway and the U.K. have already taken such initiatives.

– **Deploy resources strategically.** The challenge of effective implementation of equity policies often calls for additional resources – for extra numbers of students in the education system, for extra and more intensified teaching of students with learning difficulties, for facilities and materials for students with a disability, for teacher development, etc. However, numerous studies have shown that equality depends not only on the quantity of resources, but also on the quality of teachers and schools, and for the degree of co-operation between young people, teachers, parents and various community-based entities (including employers).

– **Set clear and achievable objectives.** Clear goals and priority setting, targeting, and monitoring of equity policies in the education system at all levels must be encouraged. Several such initiatives have been taken in OECD countries, but further development especially as regards follow-through will be necessary. It is important that equity is identified as an integrated part of the education institutions' broader strategies and not seen as something special, separate from the institutional mainstream of teaching.

– **Obtain reliable data.** There is a need for better data and indicators on equity issues in education and learning at regional, national and international levels. Good, reliable data and indicators can make an immediate impact on equity policies in education and learning.

– **Target adult training at disadvantaged groups.** There is clear evidence that those who have less education and are most at risk in the labour market get less adult training. Furthermore, employers often invest more resources in training their high-skilled, well-educated employees than in training low-skilled, low-educated employees. Public strategies and initiatives in adult training must therefore be targeted at those at risk. This is not an easy task because even if public training initiatives target this group, it must be taken into account that employers' part of work-related training is a significant element in most countries. However, for example, targeted, fiscal incentives can be used to encourage investment by small- and medium-sized enterprises in training or on any training directed at older workers, above forty, as it is the case in the Netherlands.

— ***Educate people with disabilities in an inclusive manner.*** Abundant research material from OECD countries shows that students with disabilities should, as far as possible, be educated in their local mainstream school. Funding models for schools and students should work to encourage regular schools to educate students with disabilities. The evidence continues to show that, on a per capita basis, inclusive systems are generally less costly to operate than segregated systems.

— ***Emphasise equal access to technology.*** As we have seen, the digital divide is rooted in broad societal and economic issues. Policy initiatives to bridge the various dimensions of the divide must therefore address a wide range of policy initiatives such as access to ICTs in schools, libraries and learning technology centres, ICT skill development and training, as well as telecommunication policies such as pricing of equipment and access costs.

— ***Strengthen policy co-operation on equity.*** Education policies alone will not be sufficient in addressing the equity challenge in society. Further progress will require more coherent, co-ordinated approaches across several sectors of public policy, including employment, welfare, health, housing, etc. ■

References

ATTALI, J. (1998), *Pour un Modèle Européen d'Enseignement*, Available on-line:
http://www.emn.fr/fran/enseignement/Attali.html.

DEPARTMENT OF EDUCATION, TRAINING AND YOUTH AFFAIRS, AUSTRALIA (1999), *Equity in Higher Education*, Higher Education Division, Department of Education, Training and Youth Affairs, Canberra, Australia.

DfEE – DEPARTMENT FOR EDUCATION AND EMPLOYMENT (1999), *Youth Cohort Study: The Activities and Experiences of 18 Year Olds: England and Wales 1998*, DfEE's Statistical Bulletin No. 5/99, London.

DfEE (2000), *Race Research for the Future, Ethnicity in Education, Training and the Labour Market*, Nottingham. Available on-line: http://www.dfee.gov.uk/research/.

FÖRSTER, M.F. (2000), "Trends and Driving Factors in Income Distribution and Poverty in the OECD Area", Labour Market and Social Policy Occasional Papers No. 42, OECD, Paris.

GOVERNMENT STATISTICAL SERVICE, UNITED KINGDOM (1999), *Youth Cohort Study: The Activities and Experiences of 18 Year Olds. England and Wales 1998*. Available on-line: http://www.dfee.gov.uk/statistics/DB/SBU/b0052/index.html

HEA – HIGHER EDUCATION AUTHORITY IRELAND (2000a), *Access and Equity in Higher Education, An International Perspective on Issues and Strategies*, Dublin.

HEA (2000b), *Social Background of Higher Education Entrants*, Dublin.

HEALY, T. and **ISTANCE, D.** (2000), "International Equity Indicators in Education and Learning in Industrialized Democracies: Some Recent Results and Avenues for the Future", in Douglas R. Cochrane (ed.), *In Pursuit of Equity*, Kluwer Academic Publishers, Doordrecht, the Netherlands.

HUMAN RESOURCES DEVELOPMENT CANADA (2000), *The Dual Digital Divide The Information Highway in Canada*, Ottawa.

HUTMACHER, W. (2000), "Towards a System of Equality and Equity Indicators", Working Paper.

IEA/SITES (1999), *ICT and the Emerging Paradigm for Life Long Learning: a World-wide Educational Assessment of Infrastructure, Goals and Practices*, Twente.

INSEE – INSTITUT NATIONAL DE LA STATISTIQUE ET DES ÉTUDES ÉCONOMIQUES (2000), *France, Portrait Social*, Paris.

KLASEN, S. (1999), "Social Exclusion, Children, and Education: Conceptual and Measurement Issues", background paper for the OECD.

NATIONAL STATISTICS, UK (2000), *Internet Access*, 1st Quarter 2000, London.

NCES – NATIONAL CENTRE FOR EDUCATION STATISTICS (1999), *Students with Disabilities in Post secondary Education: A Profile of Preparation, Participation, and Outcomes*. Available on-line: http://nces.ed.gov/pubs99/1999187.pdf.

NCES (2000a), *Digest of Education Statistics 1999*. Available on-line: http://nces.ed.gov/pubs2000/digest99.

NCES (2000b), *The Condition of Education 2000*. Available on-line: http://nces.ed.gov/pubs2000/coe2000/.

NCES (2000c), "Quick Tables and Figures". Available on-line: http://nces.ed.gov/quicktables.

NTIA – NATIONAL TELECOMMUNICATIONS & INFORMATION ADMINISTRATION (1999), *Falling Through the Net: Defining the Digital Divide*, U.S Department of Commerce, Washington. Available on-line: http://www.ntia.doc.gov/ntiahome/digitaldivide.

NTIA (2000), *Falling Through the Net: Toward Digital Inclusion*, U.S Department of Commerce, Washington. Available on-line: http://www.ntia.doc.gov/ntiahome/digitaldivide.

OECD (1994), *The OECD Job Study, Evidence and Explanations*, Part II, Paris.

OECD (1997a), *Education and Equity in OECD Countries*, CERI, Paris.

OECD (1997b), *Societal Cohesion and the Globalising Economy – What does the Future hold?*, Paris.

OECD (1997c), *Post-compulsory Education for Disabled People*, CERI, Paris.

OECD (1998a), *Employment Outlook*, Paris.

OECD (1998b), *Human Capital Investment – An International Comparison*, CERI, Paris.

OECD (1999a), *A Caring World – The New Social Policy Agenda*, Paris.

OECD (1999b), *Overcoming Exclusion through Adult Learning*, CERI, Paris.

OECD (1999c), *OECD Employment Outlook*, Paris.

OECD (1999d), *Education Policy Analysis 1999*, CERI, Paris.

OECD (1999e), *Inclusive Education at Work – Students with Disabilities in Mainstream Schools*, CERI, Paris.

OECD (2000a), *Education at a Glance – OECD Indicators*, CERI, Paris.

OECD (2000b), *OECD Information Technology Outlook*, Paris.

OECD (2000c), *Learning to Bridge the Digital Divide*, CERI, Paris.

OECD (2000d), *Special Needs: Statistics and Indicators*, CERI, Paris.

OECD (2000e), *Motivating Students for Lifelong Learning*, CERI, Paris.

OECD (2000f), *From Initial Education to Working Life: Making Transitions Work*, Paris.

OECD (2001a), *Cities and Regions in the New Learning Economy*, CERI, Paris.

OECD (2001b), "Understanding the Digital Divide", free document, Paris.

OECD and **STATISTICS CANADA** (2000), *Literacy in the Information Age: Final Report of the International Adult Literacy Survey*, Paris.

POST-SECONDARY EDUCATION OPPORTUNITY (1998), *Educational Opportunity by Family Income 1970 to 1996*, N° 75, September 1998, Iowa.

RITZEN, J. (2000), "Social Cohesion, Public Policy, and Economic Growth: Implications for OECD Countries", keynote address prepared for an international symposium on "The Contribution of Human and Social Capital to Sustained Economic Growth and Well-Being", Quebec, March 19-21.

RODRIGUES, M.J., SOETE, L., LINDLEY, R.M., ESPING-ANDERSEN, G., BOYER, R. and **CASTELLS, M.** (2000), "Employment, Economic Reforms and Social Cohesion – for a Europe of Innovation and Knowledge", Reports prepared for the Portuguese Presidency of the European Union.

SCHNITZER, K. *et al.* (1999), "Student Life in Germany: The Socio-Economic Picture", Summary of the 15th Social Survey of the Deutsches Studenterenwerk (DSW), Bundesministerium for Bildung und Forschung, Bonn.

SUTTON TRUST (2000), *Entry to Leading Universities*. Available on-line: http://www.suttontrust.com/text/Report1.doc.

THE ECONOMIST (06/03/00), "Back to Class War", United Kingdom.

U.S. DEPARTMENT OF EDUCATION and **OECD** (1998), *How Adults Learn*, Proceedings of a conference held April 6-8, 1998, Georgetown University Conference Centre, Washington, D.C.

WOLFE, B. and **HAVEMAN, R.** (2000), "Accounting for the Social and Non-market Benefits of Education", prepared for an international symposium on "The Contribution of Human and Social Capital to Sustained Economic Growth and Well-Being", Quebec, March 19-21.

WRIGHT, A. (2000), "Meeting the Skills Needs of Individuals and Employers in the Knowledge Economy", Paper for Learning 2010 Seminars by University for Industry and the Further Development Agency.

COMPETENCIES FOR THE KNOWLEDGE ECONOMY

SUMMARY

Pressures to increase the role of information and knowledge in national economies have provoked a wide-ranging debate about what kinds of competencies young people and adults now need.

The workforce is "upskilling", both in terms of the average educational level of workers and the types of job that they are performing. White-collar, high-skilled jobs are driving employment growth. This is not just a question of the growth in knowledge "sectors". Work is becoming more skilled across industries and within individual occupations.

A group of "knowledge workers" can be identified as those performing knowledge-rich jobs. Such workers are typically but not universally well educated. Some knowledge workers have high levels of literacy and lower levels of education, implying that basic skills obtained beyond education are recognised in the knowledge economy.

There are additional "workplace competencies" needed in the knowledge economy. Communication skills, problem-solving skills, the ability to work in teams and ICT skills, among others, are becoming important and complementary to basic core or foundation skills. Even more than other workers, knowledge workers rely on workplace competencies.

However, further research is needed to inform education policy makers about how to develop the right skills for a knowledge economy, rather than assuming that high levels of education alone, as conventionally defined, will be enough.

*This chapter examines what
is known about
competencies needed in the
knowledge economy ...*

1. INTRODUCTION

The emergence of the knowledge economy, partly attributed to globalisation and technological advances, has ushered in a wide ranging debate about the demand for higher levels of competencies. While there is growing agreement on the importance of skills *per se* as a key engine for economic growth (OECD, 2000*f*) and the spread of the knowledge economy, there is far less agreement on which competencies and skills make the difference. Within and outside of the education sector, the discourse often refers to higher educational attainment in general, focused on the development of broadly-based competencies that can support further lifelong learning. From a labour market perspective, there is also an increased attention given to specific competencies such as the ability to use information and communication technologies (ICT), to solve problems, to work in teams, to supervise and lead and to undertake continuous learning. If not necessarily new, these so-called "workplace competencies" now tend in the wider public debate to be distinguished from what is taught and learned in the course of regular schooling and tertiary education study programmes.

*... including the role of
education and literacy as
well as "workplace
competencies".*

What kinds of competencies are important for success in the knowledge economy? This chapter seeks to inform the on-going debate by trying to answer some questions related to the competencies required to participate effectively in the knowledge economy. Such an understanding is important for reforming curricula, developing appropriate assessments and providing the kinds of incentives most likely to promote the development of needed competencies.

– Section 2 surveys evidence on how the demand for competencies appears to be evolving in response to the forces at play.
– Section 3 surveys the literature to offer evidence on the different types of competencies required to participate in the knowledge economy:
  • It reviews the importance of basic education and literacy skills in the knowledge economy and for so-called "knowledge workers".
  • It analyses the extent to which further "workplace competencies" are becoming commonplace.
– Section 4 draws together what is known about the demand for competencies in the knowledge economy, drawing attention to information gaps and needs.

2. THE KNOWLEDGE REVOLUTION

2.1 Technological change and ICTs

*The knowledge economy is
based on the production and
use of information and
knowledge ...,*

The concepts of "knowledge economy" and "knowledge worker" are based on the view that information and knowledge are at the centre of economic growth and development. The ability to produce and use information effectively is thus a vital source of skills for many individuals (OECD, 2000*e*).

*... driven partly by
possibilities opened up
through technological
change.*

Technological change and innovation drive the development of the knowledge-based economy through their effects on production methods, consumption patterns and the structure of economies. Both are closely related in recent growth performance. Some changes in innovation processes could not have occurred without ICTs and conversely, some of the impact of ICTs might not have been felt in the absence of changes in the innovation system (OECD, 2000*a*). These changes also have affected the way in which organisations interact in the economy, with networking, co-operation and the fluid flow of knowledge within and across national borders gaining in importance.

Efforts are currently underway at the OECD to learn more about the effects of ICTs and other factors on recent growth patterns. Preliminary findings point towards technology and innovation as important drivers of recent economic growth performance (OECD, 2000a). Other work has also identified techno-logical change as an important determinant of employment growth (Blanchflower et al., 1991) and of increased demand for more highly educated and skilled workers (Berman et al., 1997; Kiley, 1999; Machin et al., 1996).

Knowledge-based industries, which include the main producers of high-technology goods, high- and medium-high technology manufacturing and the main users of technology (namely knowledge-intensive services such as finance, insurance, business, communication and community, social and personal services), account for more than half of OECD GDP and continue to grow rapidly (OECD, 2000g). As shown in Figure 4.1, the share of knowledge-based industries and services in business-sector value added and in employment increased over the past decade in almost all countries.

Knowledge-based industries already account for more than half of OECD GDP.

Figure 4.1 Increasing importance of knowledge-based industries, 1985 and 1997

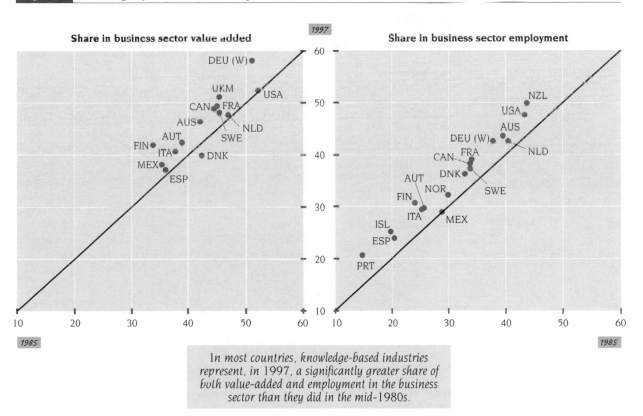

In most countries, knowledge-based industries represent, in 1997, a significantly greater share of both value-added and employment in the business sector than they did in the mid-1980s.

Countries above the diagonal are those for which knowledge-based industries' share of value-added or employment was greater in 1997 than in 1985.

Source: OECD (2000), *Science, Technology and Industry Outlook.* ....

Data for Figure 4.1, p. 150.

The growth of knowledge-based industries is taking place at a time of increased investment in ICTs and growth in the use of the Internet. Investment in IT hardware, software and services and telecommunications accounted for almost 7% of OECD GDP in 1997, with the highest shares in Sweden, the United States, the United Kingdom, Switzerland, Australia, Japan, New Zealand and Canada. In the two years prior to 1997, investment increased by 13% in real terms.

2.2 Upskilling of the labour force

Globalisation, changes in technology and organisations are altering the demands for different types of labour...

To adapt and maintain competitiveness in response to changing consumer preferences and technological change, companies need appropriate organisational structures, a skilled workforce and able management. These changes are having a significant impact on the structure of employment and on the type of labour required. The most obvious manifestation of this is the rising human capital levels of the populations and workforces in OECD countries, as measured by educational attainment and as implied by an increased demand for more highly-educated and highly-skilled workers.[1]

Over the past generation, as documented in Chapter 2 of this volume, the proportion of adults in OECD countries with at least secondary-level education

| Figure 4.2 | Growth in the proportion of the population and employment with tertiary-level qualifications, 1989-96 |

Percentage point change in the share of individuals with tertiary education

In many OECD countries, the share of workers with tertiary education has increased more rapidly than the share of the population educated at this level.

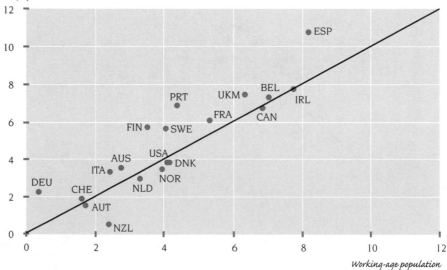

Countries above the diagonal are those in which the growth of people with tertiary education has been more rapid in employment than in the working-age population.

Source: OECD (2000), *Economic Outlook*.

Data for Figure 4.2, p. 150.

1. A number of recent and ongoing OECD efforts seek to develop better definitions and measures of skills: the International Adult Literacy Survey (IALS), the programme on Definition and Selection of Competencies: Theoretical and Conceptual Foundations (DeSeCo), and the Adult Literacy and Life Skills (ALL) survey.

| Figure 4.3 | Upskilling in total employment growth, 1980-98 |

Average annual percentage change in total employment

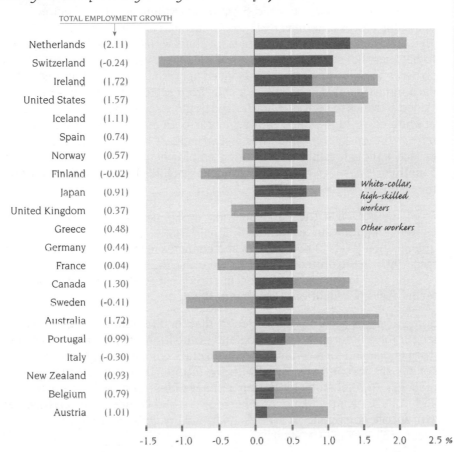

TOTAL EMPLOYMENT GROWTH

Employment is being driven by white-collar, high-skilled jobs in almost all countries.

Countries are ranked in descending order of average annual percentage growth in white-collar, high-skilled workers.
Sources: ILO database (2000) and OECD (1998), *Technology, Productivity and Job Creation.*
Data for Figure 4.3, p. 150.

has risen, on average, from 44% to 72%, and the share with at least tertiary education has almost doubled, from 22% to 41% (OECD, 2000c). This is largely due to the increase in the educational attainment of younger generations, which has contributed to widen differences between younger and older adults in almost all OECD countries.

Evidence that upskilling is taking place is indicated by a bias in most OECD countries towards better educated individuals in the labour market. Figure 4.2 shows the changes in the proportion of persons with tertiary education in employment and the changes in their share in the total working-age population. The fact that most countries are located above the diagonal reveals that labour markets over the 1990s have benefited from more highly educated workers.

... manifested in a more highly educated workforce ...

Figure 4.3 illustrates the importance of this upskilling in accounting for employment growth. Over the past two decades, in 14 out of 21 countries for which data are available, growth in the professional, technical, administra-

... and more rapid growth in white-collar, high-skilled occupations.

tive and managerial occupations ("white-collar, high-skilled") has increased more than employment in other occupational categories.

Upskilling, in terms of the growth of white collar, high skill jobs, is evident both within manufacturing and service sectors ...

More detailed analyses of employment trends within industries confirm a true upskilling process (Berman *et al.*, 1997; Machin *et al.*, 1996; Steedman, 1998). Those studies suggest that employment shifts within industries, as opposed to between industries, represent a real change towards higher skills. This is so because it reflects a rather generalised upskilling process occurring within each industry rather than solely a shift from sectors characterised by low-skilled activities to sectors characterised by more skilled activities. The growth of white-collar, high-skilled employment in both manufacturing and services reflects this upskilling, rather than just an increase in service sector activities. In fact, although total manufacturing employment has decreased in most countries, it has increased for white-collar, high-skilled occupations within the sector.

... and within individual occupations.

From another angle, there appears to be upskilling within occupations. Two United Kingdom surveys show a considerable increase in the average qualification levels of new recruits and an increase in job complexity (Green *et al.*, 1997). In the United States, jobs were also found to require higher levels of skills than in the past within occupations, especially in professional and technological occupations (Osterman, 1995).

Some analyses go further. They report that, in addition to upskilling of the labour force in terms of education and occupation, there is also a new and distinct demand for a certain set of "workplace competencies" and "interpersonal skills" usually associated with the introduction of ICTs and new work practices. Several studies (Section 3.2) have identified these competencies and skills as team-working, problem-solving and communication, together with specific computing skills (Bresnahan and Brynjolfsson, 1999; Green, 1998; Green *et al.*, 2000; Stasz, 2000).

So, upskilling and a growing demand for diversified competencies are key features of the knowledge economy.

3. WHAT COMPETENCIES ARE DISTINCTIVE IN THE KNOWLEDGE ECONOMY?

Although there is no clear agreement on the specific competencies needed for the knowledge economy ...

How should education and training systems respond to on-going changes in the knowledge economy that demand higher and more diversified skills? This is a difficult question to answer because there is no clear agreement on the definition and measurement of these skills and on how such skills contribute to the knowledge economy. One way to approach this issue is to examine the different evidence available on general competency trends and on how these can be related to the knowledge economy.

... both basic skills and other non-academic skills are now required for improved job performance...

Some analysts suggest that basic reading, writing and arithmetic skills are no longer enough for workplace performance (Carnevale *et al.*, 1990), but they are the starting point. Further findings stress the fact that there are new or changing competencies which are highly valued in the labour market. In addition to basic foundation or core skills based on formal education and literacy, other non-academic skills are being widely included in the literature as important and as part of a multidimensional vision of skills (Stasz and Brewer, 1999).

Table 4.1 **Employers' hiring criteria in the United States, 1994 and 1997**

Employers' responses to the question: "After you have established your applicant pool and obtained information about potential (job title) employees, what characteristics or attributes are most critical in making your hiring decision?"	Average of responses on a scale of 1 to 5: 1 = not at all important; ... to 5 = essential	
Characteristics	1994	1997
Applicant's attitude	4.6	4.6
Applicant's communication skills	4.2	4.1
Previous employer references	3.4	3.9
Previous work experience	4.0	3.8
Industry based credentials	3.2	3.2
Years of completed schooling	2.9	2.9
Academic performance	2.5	2.5
Score on tests administered as part of the interview	2.5	2.3
Teacher recommendations	2.1	2.0
Experience or reputation of applicant's school	2.4	2.0

Source: Shapiro *et al.* (1998)

In hiring decisions, employers say they give as much attention to workplace competencies as they do to technical skills. However, most of the available surveys refer to hiring at a particular level, requiring a given level of education as a first prerequisite. From this perspective, the focus on intra-personal and workplace competencies should be seen as supplementary to the established educational requirements. In the United States, a qualitative survey on firms' recruitment strategies for entry-level jobs found that not only mathematical and English skills were required for today's entry-level jobs, but intra-personal skills were also quite important (Rosenbaum and Binder, 1997). Table 4.1, based on data from the National Employer Survey (run in 1994 and 1997), shows that among the hiring criteria for potential employees, intra-personal and communication skills were the highest ranked, followed by work experience. In the United Kingdom, employers reported that communication skills, learning ability, problem-solving skills, team work and the capacity for self-management were more important than technical, ICT or numeracy skills as criteria in the recruitment of graduates (Hesketh, 2000). Employers placed high importance on inter-personal and intra-personal skills and gave rather less weight to narrower, learned skills. According to the employers surveyed, initiative, motivation and communication skills were considered as particularly relevant, because a motivated new hire easily could obtain the necessary specific skills through training or on-the-job experience (Industry in Education, 1996).

... and employers give us much attention in hiring decisions to general workplace competencies as to specialised job skills at given levels of education ...

Box 4.1 **Workplace competencies**

A literature review reveals that the different types of workplace competencies that are most agreed upon by different analysts, surveys and country reports are:

Inter-personal skills:
- Team work and the ability to collaborate in pursuit of a common objective.
- Leadership capabilities.

Intra-personal skills:
- Motivation and attitude.
- The ability to learn.
- Problem-solving skills.
- Effective communication with colleagues and clients.
- Analytical skills.

Technological or ICT *skills.*

For further reading, refer to Stasz (2000).

... with some countries' skills or qualifications frameworks distinguishing between workplace competencies and foundation or core skills.

In some countries, workplace competencies have been defined within frameworks in which these competencies are distinguished from core or foundation skills. Examples include the United States' SCANS competencies (Wise *et al.*, 1990), the Australian key competencies (Australian Education Council, 1993), and the Conference Board of Canada's employability skills profile (Conference Board of Canada, 1992) or the United Kingdom's National Curriculum for Vocational Qualifications (QCA, 1997). Most of these reports agree on a certain set of skills that are also stressed in employer surveys and observation of workplace practices (ERT, 1995) (See Box 4.1).

In the same vein as these reports, the rest of this section distinguishes between academic and cognitive skills and workplace competencies, based on a view that the former are the core or foundation skills that workers require. Workplace competencies are viewed as complementary for participating in the knowledge economy and in new production processes. The analysis focuses on so-called "knowledge workers" (Box 4.2), *i.e.* those workers who are participating most effectively in the knowledge economy, on the grounds that their competencies strongly reflect the emerging dynamics of technological change and globalisation.

3.1 Knowledge workers are highly educated and/or highly literate

Knowledge workers typically have a high level of initial education and/or a good level of literacy (see Technical Annex at the end of the chapter). On one hand, the recognition of formal knowledge obtained upon leaving the initial education and training system can provide the basis for becoming a knowledge worker through the recruitment process which, in most OECD countries, very often depends heavily on official certificates. At the same time, individuals can obtain the required competencies to be designated as knowledge workers through experience, training or more informal ways, well-documented in the literature about informal or non-formal learning.

Box 4.2 **Different definitions of knowledge workers**

The term "knowledge worker" has been coined to describe those workers who are participating most effectively in the knowledge-based economy. However, if the definition of the knowledge economy is challenging, so is that of the knowledge worker. It can be people who are working in knowledge-based sectors or workers who have specific skills and competencies. At the heart of all the suggested definitions lies the idea that knowledge workers are participating in the utilisation and creation of knowledge. Different definitions of high-skilled or knowledge workers use a combination or reclassification of the different occupational measures available:

— Symbolic analyst

Reich (1991) distinguishes the "symbolic analytic services" from direct personal services and routine production services. Workers in the first of these categories are professionals, upper-middle managers and above, and others who create, modify, and synthesise knowledge. Such workers account for about 20% of the U.S. labour force.

— Science and technology (ST) personnel as high-skilled workers

According to the OECD *Canberra Manual on the Measurement of Human Resources Devoted to Science and Technology* (OECD, 1995), there are different ways to classify science and technology workers. Science and technology personnel comprise those who are either highly educated or employed in occupations requiring at least a first university degree. By combining qualification and occupation, the definition identifies both education and skills needed for different types of jobs (Cervantes, 1999).

— Knowledge worker according to new occupational groupings

According to Lavoie and Roy (1998), the main feature of a knowledge-based economy is the increasing need to rely on highly-skilled workers whose skills are not exclusively related to science and technology but also to the control, management and co-ordination of tasks. To define knowledge workers, they reformulate occupational categories based on the use and production of knowledge by workers and reclassify economic activities according to tasks performed by workers (from the more conventional industrial activies). Drawing on Osberg *et al.* (1989), they regroup occupational categories in five domains: knowledge, management, data, services and goods. Knowledge occupations, under this definition, account from 7.9% of the labour force in Portugal to 25.4% in Finland (OECD, 2001).

— Knowledge worker by occupations and tasks

Knowledge workers are defined according to their occupation and tasks for the purpose of this chapter. Specifically, knowledge workers are those employed in occupations considered to be white-collar, high-skilled *and* perform a set of tasks that revolve around creating and processing information (reading, writing and quantitative tasks). The Technical Annex provides further details on the definition and measurement of knowledge workers using the International Adult Literacy Survey (IALS). According to this definition, knowledge workers account for an estimated 18.6% of the labour force in those OECD countries participating in IALS, ranging from 6.4% in Poland to 25.5% in Sweden.

*Those who are more highly
educated are more likely to
be knowledge workers,
particularly those who have
followed broadly-based
academic studies
throughout...*

Analyses based on the International Adult Literacy Survey (IALS) data confirm this (see Technical Annex). Among adults who test at similar literacy levels and share other common characteristics, those who are more highly educated are more likely to be knowledge workers. Indeed, those with more years of education (excluding repeated years) are *ceteris paribus* more likely to be knowledge workers. However, those with vocational preparation at the upper secondary level, even if they continue on to tertiary education, are less likely to be knowledge workers. This suggests that the competencies needed for the knowledge economy are likely to be more broadly-based rather than narrowly vocational.

*... but also those with high
literacy skills are more likely
to be knowledge workers ...*

But, analyses of the IALS data also show that those who have higher levels of literacy are more likely to be knowledge workers. This applies regardless of the level or years of education. So, skills and competencies acquired through means other than formal education can be important.[2] Moreover, generally, knowledge workers are highly skilled in *any* type of literacy skill.[3]

Table 4.2 **Education and literacy skills of knowledge workers**

Proportion of knowledge workers by education and literacy levels

	Educational attainment (%)		
	Upper secondary and below	Tertiary	Total
Literacy			
Levels 1/2	6.9	3.7	10.6
Level 3	20.0	17.5	37.5
Levels 4/5	17.1	34.8	51.9
Total	44.0	56.0	100.0

Source: International Adult Literacy Survey (1994-98).

*... and about one in five
knowledge workers lack
advanced educational
qualifications, but have high
literacy skills.*

As presented in Table 4.2, about one-third (34.8%) of knowledge workers are, at the same time, highly educated (completed some tertiary education) and highly literate.[4] Moreover, 73% of knowledge workers are either highly educated *or* highly literate (as highlighted in blue in the table). So, knowledge workers may well acquire the necessary skills and competencies to be a knowledge worker through means other than formal education. In fact, knowledge workers are also more likely to participate in training. An estimated 67% undertook training in the last year before the survey, compared to a 41%

---

2. Having reached only secondary education, a man can increase his possibility of being a knowledge worker to that of somebody who has upper secondary education by increasing his literacy score by 49 points, and to that of somebody with tertiary education with 74 points (on a scale from 0 to 500). For women, the differences are larger.

3. The findings do not vary markedly according to differences in performance among the three literacy scales – prose, document and quantitative. The main exception is that men who score lowest on the prose or quantitative scales are less likely to be knowledge workers than men who score lowest on the document scale.

4. That is, perform at the top levels (4 or 5) on the literacy scale.

training rate for all other workers. In this connection, participation in training can be viewed as both a consequence and a cause of being a knowledge worker: such workers are more likely to receive training, but they are also more likely to be skilled which can reflect in part a prior disposition toward training.

3.2 Workplace competencies

Workplace competencies refer to a set of skills that are complementary to academic or more technical skills. As noted above, employers report that they give weight to these skills in hiring decisions and more generally such skills appear to be required for workers to function effectively within the new organisational structures adopted by leading-edge firms. To the degree that most of these studies link these requirements to recent economic developments and the demand for a highly skilled workforce, it seems reasonable to assume that they can also be associated with the knowledge-based economy.

Indeed, this interpretation is consistent with the literature. Reich's (1991) definition of knowledge workers refers to the ability for problem-identifying, problem-solving and strategic brokering capabilities. A main characteristic of knowledge workers, apart from having tertiary education, is that facts are not central to their skills profiles because whatever data are required will be available to them at the touch of a computer key. The more important skill these workers bring to their work is an ability to conceptualise problems and solutions. Reich calls for attention to the development of four basic skills: abstraction, system thinking, experimentation and collaboration.

Further evidence on the use of workplace competencies by knowledge workers is provided by an analysis of detailed occupational data for the Canadian workforce. This assesses the degree to which knowledge workers are more likely than other workers to use cognitive, communication and management skills. Figure 4.4 shows that knowledge workers (according to the "new occupational groupings" definition; see Box 4.2) have much higher average scores than the rest of Canadian workforce for cognitive skills, people skills (direct and team-work) and communication skills (Béjaoui, 2000). These are some of the skill domains frequently identified for those working in a knowledge-based economy (Massé et al., 1998).

Most of these workplace competencies have been related to new work organisation practices. Such practices include job rotation, team-based work organisation, greater involvement of lower-level employees and flattened management structures (OECD, 1999a). Some analyses have found that, as different new work organisation practices are set into motion, the use of different workplace competencies increases (Green et al., 2000).

Organisational changes taking place in the service sector, which employs the largest proportions of knowledge workers, provide further support for these findings. A 1988 survey of developments in France, Germany, Japan, Sweden and the United States showed then that the emergence of the new workplace environment was accompanied by greater demands for competencies specifically to cope with the changes being introduced: the ability to operate in an unclear and ever-changing environment, the capacity to deal with non-

Workplace competencies are linked to the ability to function effectively in firms that have adopted new work practices …

… which requires abstraction, system thinking, experimentation and collaboration skills, according to Reich …

… while a Canadian analysis identifies communication and management skills along with cognitive skills as the domains knowledge workers use more than other workers.

Such workplace competencies are needed as new work practices are introduced …

… in the service sector …

COMPETENCIES FOR THE
KNOWLEDGE ECONOMY

Knowledge workers in
Canada require much
more cognitive,
management and
communication skills than
other workers.

Figure 4.4   Skill requirements of knowledge workers in five domains,[1] Canada

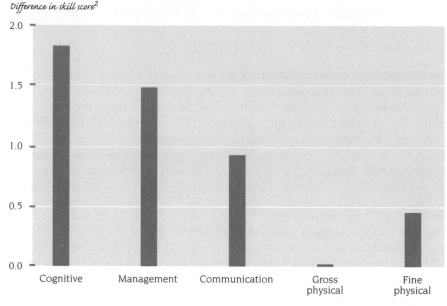

Difference in skill score[2]

Skill domains

1. The scoring is based on the Canadian Classification and Dictionary of Occupations (CCDO) which give scores to 6 500 occupations according to the requirements of the job. There are 43 indices representing general education, physical abilities and other different aptitudes. Running a Principal Component Analysis gives a clustering of the indices and each cluster represents a specific skill.

2. The score is the difference between the average score of knowledge workers and the average score of all workers.

Source: Béjaoui (2000), *Sur la mesure des qualifications.*
Data for Figure 4.4, p. 150.

routine and abstract work processes, the ability to handle decisions and responsibilities, group and interactive work and system-wide or broad understanding (Bertrand and Noyelle, 1988). The study also suggested the need for better interaction and communication skills for all workers, stronger abilities to work in group situations and more workers with high levels of specialised professional expertise and entrepreneurship, especially among middle-level professional and managerial personnel.

... and in public utilities, among other industries.

A study of practices in production work by those employed in public utilities in the United States concluded that greater use of innovative work practices increased the need for higher skill levels and workplace competencies (Capelli and Rogovski, 1994). Those competencies most commonly required by new work practices are team work, communication skills, problem-solving and analytical skills. Although new work practices may lead to greater demands on workers' technical skills, the study further concluded that the new practices appear to focus more on workplace competencies than specific technical or vocational skills. Similar findings are reported in a study of commercial vehicle manufacturing (Thompson *et al*,. 1995). This study found that increases in new forms of production led to growing demand for organisational and technological knowledge and the ability to work in teams, with an emphasis on behavioural or "extra-functional" skills. Findings from a survey of German employers provides yet more support for the view that workplace competencies are required for modern work processes (Dybowski, 1998).

New work practices have also been associated with the introduction and greater use of technology on the job, in firms and in the economy. Apparently, these changes have implications for the levels and types of workplace competencies. Analyses carried out on firm-level practices show a strong correlation between information technology, human capital and workplace organisation (Bresnahan and Brynjolfsson, 1999; OECD, 1999*a*). Other studies have found links between the introduction of ICTs and the demand for skills or skills upgrading (Baldwin *et al.*, 1997; Berman *et al.*, 1997; Machin *et al.*, 1996). All of these studies find evidence of capital-skill complementarity and strong positive correlations between the level of computer investment in an industry and changes in the skill composition of the workforce.

New work practices – and upskilling – have also followed the introduction and greater use of technology in enterprises and sectors...

To further analyse the aspect of ICT skills demand, a distinction can be made between workers employed in ICT industries and workers in other sectors who may need to acquire ICT skills to function effectively in their jobs or everyday life. With respect to the latter, demand for ICT skills appears to be growing in all sectors of the economy and society and not only for knowledge workers. Some experts suggest that as democratisation of ICTs takes place, workers may be required to have the necessary generic skills for acquiring, through short training spells,[5] ever-changing ICT skills requirements (OECD, 1999*b*). The response needed to meet this challenge may, in fact, be a matter of balance. The Skill Survey of the Employed British Workforce found that, in most cases, people easily acquire the necessary computer skills when computers are introduced. The study goes on to conclude that a possible over-investment in computer skills may mask shortcomings regarding other skills that can be more crucial for the job. According to the authors, although computers have contributed to changes in the demand for skills in the labour market, computer skills *per se* do not play a key role in this process (Borghans and Weel, 2000).[6]

... but while the demand for specific ICT skills appears to be growing in all sectors and for all workers, such skills are relatively easily acquired ...

5. One study estimates that about one-half of all computer users in France received some specialised computer training. Such training exceeded one week for about one-quarter of all users (Gollac and Kramarz, 1997).

6. There is an unresolved debate about the impact of computers on wages. One British study suggests that people with computer skills obtain wage premiums in excess of 20%, although it is not clear whether the premiums are due to higher overall skills of the workers who use computers (Green, 1998). Another study found that workers who used computers obtained wages about one-third (36%) higher than others, although the increment is not a direct return to computer skills. Instead, computer skills are associated with other competencies, such as basic education and generate certain non-wage benefits, identified as better integration in the firm or improved professional recognition. The data are for 1993 and refer to France (Gollac and Kramarz, 1997). Some studies of workers find not only a strong association between higher levels of education and computer skills, but also that those with higher levels of education are more productive in the use of ICTs (Krueger, 1993; Autor *et al.*, 1997). In Germany, wage premiums have been associated with handwriting as well as with computer use (DiNardo and Pischke, 1997), while in Canada wage premiums were found for computer and fax use (Morissette and Drolet, 1997). These results suggest that the returns to computer use reflect unobserved characteristics of workers or of the nature of their work.

*... so even ICT-intensive
firms seek in their employees
a broader combination of
technical, business,
management and personal
skills.*

ICT-intensive firms in particular seek a combination of technical, business and management and personal skills (among which communication, leadership, team work and problem-solving skills) (OECD, 2000d). This conclusion is supported by findings from studies in a number of OECD countries: United States (NRC, 2000; ITAA, 2000), Canada (ACST, 2000; Sangster, 1999), Ireland (ISC, 2000) and the United Kingdom (DfEE, 2000). A further finding of interest is that workers entering ICT jobs now develop, certify and present qualifications through private firms, business associations and commercial ICT bodies as much as through ICT study programmes in schools, colleges and universities (Adelman, 2000).

4. CONCLUSIONS

*This analysis suggests that
while further increases in the
levels of education are
needed, for knowledge
workers and others ...*

The development of the knowledge economy is changing labour market demands for competencies and skills. There is evidence that upskilling has taken place throughout OECD economies, partly derived by an increase in demand for skills and partly in response to rising educational attainments in populations. The forces at play suggest that further increases in the overall levels of education are needed. Higher levels of education are needed not only just to better prepare knowledge workers. They also improve the likelihood of participation in further learning throughout adult life, and reduce the chances of long-term unemployment and marginalisation.

*... knowledge workers also
need a wider range of
competencies ...*

At the same time, many commentators have argued that new or additional competencies and skills are required from workers. On the basis of evidence available on general trends in competencies and on their relation to the knowledge economy, we conclude that high levels of education and literacy are the key principal competencies demanded in the knowledge economy. Basic general education provides workers with the core academic and cognitive competencies required to participate most effectively. These core competencies provide the base to facilitate further training and further upgrading of those specific technical skills required for knowledge workers.

Knowledge workers, *i.e.* those in jobs requiring the production and use of knowledge, require high levels of competencies and skills. These are not delineated solely in terms of educational attainment: almost one in five knowledge workers lack advanced formal qualifications but demonstrate high literacy skills. To some extent, knowledge workers have acquired and are applying relevant, advanced levels of skills not developed through formal education – a finding which seems to apply more to men than to women.

*... including workplace
competencies of team-work,
communication skills and
problem-solving skills.*

There are other competencies that, although not necessarily new, are now seen to be more important for knowledge workers. For example, so-called "workplace competencies", *e.g.* team-work, communication skills and problem-solving skills, have been associated with new organisation practices and knowledge workers. These workplace competencies are not seen as substitutes for education and literacy skills, but rather as complementary to them. Moreover, the extent to which these competencies are developed independently or are convex to educational attainment, on-the-job training and/or off-the-job training remains unclear.

In the light of these questions, policy directions are less clear. Improving the educational foundations, literacy skills and ICT literacy for everyone seems warranted. But, more research is needed to justify and guide substantial changes in the context, contents and methods of teaching and learning aimed at developing new competencies and skills. ■

Further research is needed to improve understanding of how and where needed competencies are best developed.

TECHNICAL ANNEX

1. Definition of knowledge workers using the International Adult Literacy Survey (IALS)

The definition of knowledge workers used in this chapter relies on occupations and tasks performed most often at work as measured in the International Adult Literacy Survey (IALS).They are identified on the basis of responses to two sets of questions in the IALS background questionnaire.

The first set of questions has to do with the tasks workers do on a regular basis. These tasks revolve around processing information or documents (reading, writing and mathematics) and are considered good proxies for assessing what people do at work. The second set of questions includes workers' occupations on a one-digit coding.

In relation to tasks, the questions are:

The following questions refer to the job at which you worked the most hours in the last 12 months.

E1. How often (do/did) you read or use information from each of the following as part of your main job? Would you say every day, a few times a week, once a week, less than once a week, rarely or never?

– Letter or memos

– Reports, articles, magazines or journals

– Manuals or reference books, including catalogues

– Material written in a language other than the mother tongue of the person

E2. How often (do/did) you write or fill out each of the following as part of your main job? Would you say every day, a few times a week, once a week, less than once a week, rarely or never?

– Letter or memos

– Reports or articles

– Estimates or technical specifications

E3. In your main job, how often do you use arithmetic or mathematics (that is, adding, subtracting, multiplying or dividing) to:

– calculate prices, costs or budgets?

For each item, those answering "Every day" are given a score of 10 points; those answering "A few times a week", 5 points; followed by 3, 2 and 1 point for "Rarely or never". The scores are added up with a maximum score of 80 (doing everything "Every day") and a minimum of 8 (doing everything "Rarely or never").

In relation to occupations, the question is:

What kind of work were you doing at this job? (Give full description or occupational title, *e.g.* office clerk, machine operator, computer programmer)

which is coded according to ISCO:

0: Armed Forces

1: Legislators, Senior Officials and Managers

2: Professionals

3: Technicians and Associate Professionals

The worker is considered a "knowledge worker" when s/he scores 40 or above on tasks involving the use of information and is working in: the armed forces; as a legislator, senior official or manager; professional; or technician and associate professional (occupations 0, 1, 2 and 3). The value 40 on the score range between 8 and 80 represents at the same time the middle of the range and the value a worker would score if s/he were doing all the tasks "a few times a week" (8 times 5). It is also the score a worker would attain by doing 4 of the 8 tasks every day. For these reasons, the value 40 has been retained as the threshold to define a knowledge worker.

2. The Probit model

The statistical modelling used to quantify the key determinants of the probability of being a knowledge worker is based on econometric tools dealing with limited dependent variables (explained variables whose values are not continuous). In this case, the dependent variable takes on the value of 1 if the individual is a knowledge worker and 0 otherwise. The methodology adopted relies on a two-step process, with a first-step equation to control for the probability of being in the labour force in the main model.

Different specification have been tested and the final set of explanatory variables is:

- Country dummies.
- Age (continuous) and age squared.
- Born in the country or not.
- Best score in literacy (out of the three possible ones – continuous).
- Living in a rural area or not.
- Dummy for individual's best literacy score (prose, document or quantitative).
- Dummy for individual's worst literacy score (prose, document or quantitative).
- Educational attainment (5 levels).
- Number of years of schooling (not included the repetition of years – continuous).
- Type of preparation at upper secondary level (vocational, academic or other).
- Dummy for being currently unemployed.
- Training and type (occupational, personal or other reasons).
- Dummy for following a course in order to improve literacy.
- Dummies for industry where individual works or had worked (unemployed).
- Type of job (employee or self-employed, with supervision or not).
- Number of hours worked per week (continuous).
- Number of employers (continuous).

Two models are estimated by gender because the selection equation and the labour market behaviour vary according to gender. A model has been run for each country for men only. There are slight differences of explanatory variables between the different models because some variables are not present for some countries. The results of these probit estimations are available from the Secretariat on request.

Note: The goals of IALS was to develop estimates of literacy, based on performance on a common set of literacy tasks undertaken by samples of adults in 18 OECD countries. IALS collected biographical information, such as educational attainment, and details on occupations and job tasks, from each participating adult. In each participating country, samples of 2 300 to 8 000 adults were drawn to be broadly representative of the civilian, non-institutionalised population aged 16 to 65. Response rates ranged from 45% to 75% across countries. See Pont and Werquin (2000) and OECD and Statistics Canada (2000).

References

ACST – CANADIAN ADVISORY COUNCIL ON SCIENCE AND TECHNOLOGY (2000), *Stepping up: Skills and opportunities in the knowledge economy*, Report of the Expert Panel on skills. http://acst-ccst.gc.ca/acst/skills/home_e.html

ADELMAN, C. (2000), A *Parallel Postsecondary Universe: The certification system in information technology*, Office of Educational Research and Improvement, U.S. Department of Education, Washington, D.C.

AUSTRALIAN EDUCATION COUNCIL (1993), "Putting general education to work: The key competencies report", Committee to advise the Australian Education Council.

AUTOR, D., KATZ, L.F. and **KRUEGER, A.B.** (1997), "Computing Inequality: Have computers changed the labour market?", NBER working paper No. W5956, National Bureau of Economic Research, Cambridge, MA.

BALDWIN, J.R., GRAY, T. and **JONHSON, J.** (1997), "Technology Induced Wage Premia in Canadian Manufacturing Plants during the 1980s", Working Paper No. 92, Micro-Economics Analysis Division, Statistics Canada, Ottawa.

BÉJAOUI, A. (2000), *Sur la mesure des qualifications : application à l'émergence de l'économie du savoir*, Human Resources Development Canada, Ottawa.

BERMAN, E., BOUND, J. and **MACHIN, S.** (1997), "Implications of skilled-biased technological change: International evidence", NBER working paper No. 6166, National Bureau of Economic Research, Cambridge, MA.

BERTRAND, O. and **NOYELLE, T.** (1988), *Human Resources and Corporate Strategy: Technological change in banks and insurance companies*, OECD, Paris.

BLANCHFLOWER, D., MILLWARD, N. and **OSWALD, A.** (1991), "Unionism and Employment Behaviour", *Economic Journal*, Vol. 101, No. 407, pp. 815-834.

BORGHANS, L. and **WEEL, B. TER** (2000), "Do we Need Computer Skills to Use a Computer? Evidence from the UK", Draft article, Maastricht University, June.

BRESNAHAN, T.F. and **BRYNJOLFSSON, E.** (1999), "Information Technology, Workplace Organisation and the Demand for Skilled Labor: Firm-level evidence", NBER working paper No. 7136.

CAPELLI, P. and **ROGOVSKI, N.** (1994), "New Work Systems and Skill Requirements", *International Labour Review*, Vol. 133, No. 2.

CARNEVALE, A., GAINER, L. and **MELTZER, A.** (1990), *Workplace Basics: The essential skills employers want*, Jossey-Bass, San Francisco.

CERVANTES, M. (1999), "Background Report: Analysis of science and technology labour markets in OECD countries", in OECD (ed.), *Mobilising Human Resources for Innovation: Proceedings from the OECD Workshop on Science and Technology Labour Markets*, Paris, 17 May, pp. 65-77.

CONFERENCE BOARD OF CANADA (1992), *Employability Skills Profile*, http://www.conferenceboard.ca/nbec/eprof-e.htm

DfEE – UNITED KINGDOM DEPARTMENT FOR EDUCATION AND EMPLOYMENT (2000), *Skills for the Information Age*, Final Report from the Information Technology, Communication and Electronic Skills Strategy Group, http://www.dfee.gov.uk/skillsforce/index.htm

DINARDO, J.E. and **PISCHKE, J.S.** (1997), "The Returns to Computer Use Revisited: Have pencils changed the wage structure too?", *Quarterly Journal of Economics*, Vol. CXII(1), pp. 291-304.

DYBOWSKI, G. (1998), "New technologies and work organisation: impact on vocational education and training", in Tessaring, M. (ed.), *Vocational Education and Training – the European research field*, Background report 1998. Vol. 1, CEDEFOP, Thessaloniki.

ERT – EDUCATION FOR EUROPEANS (1995), *Towards the learning society. A report from the European Round Table of Industrialists*, Brussels.

GOLLAC, M. and **KRAMARZ, F.** (1997), "L'ordinateur: un outil de sélection? Utilisation de l'informatique, salaire et risque de chômage", *Revue Economique*, Vol 48, No. 5, pp. 1115-1143, Septembre.

GREEN, F. (1998), "The Value of Skills", *Studies in Economics*, No. 98/19, University of Kent at Canterbury.

GREEN, F. ASHTON, D. and **FELSTEAD, A.** (2000), "Estimating the Determinants of Supply of Computing, Problem-Solving, Communication, Social and Team-working Skills", Paper presented at the Seminar "Skills Measurement and Economic Analysis", 27-29 March, 2000, University of Kent at Canterbury, Canterbury.

GREEN, F., ASHTON, D., BURCHELL, B., DAVIES, B. and **FELSTEAD, A.** (1997), "An Analysis of Changing Work Skills in Britain", Center of Economic Performance, Discussion Paper Series, London School of Economics and Political Science.

HESKETH, A.J. (2000), "Recruiting an Elite? Employers' perceptions of graduate education and training", *Journal of Education and Work*, Vol. 13, No. 3, pp. 245-271.

INDUSTRY IN EDUCATION (1996), "Towards employability. Addressing the gap between young people's qualities and employers' recruitment needs", London.

ISC – IRELAND INFORMATION SOCIETY COMMISSION (2000), *New Technology in Irish Business: Skills and Training* (Business 3), May. http://www.infosocomm.ie

ITAA – INFORMATION TECHNOLOGY ASSOCIATION OF AMERICA (2000), *Bridging the Gap: Information Technology Skills for a New Millenium*, April. http://www.itaa.org

KILEY, M. (1999), "The Supply of Skilled Labour and Skilled biased Technological Progress", *The Economic Journal*, No. 109, October, pp. 708-724.

KRUEGER, A.B. (1993), "How Computers Have Changed the Wage Structure – Evidence from microdata, 1984-1989", *Quarterly Journal of Economics*, Vol. CVIII(1), pp. 33-60.

LAVOIE, M. and **ROY, R.** (1998), *Employment in the Knowledge-based Economy: A growth accounting exercise for Canada*, Applied Research Branch, Human Resource Development Canada, working paper R-98-8E, June.

MACHIN, S., RYAN, A. and **VAN REENAN, J.** (1996), "Technology and Changes in Skill Structure, Evidence from an International Panel of Industries", Center for Economic Performance, Discussion Paper Series, London School of Economics and Political Science.

MASSÉ, P., ROY, R. and **GINGRAS, Y.** (1998), "The Changing Skill Structure of Employment in Canada", Applied Research Branch, Human Resources Development Canada, Working paper R-99-7E, November.

MORISSETTE, R. and **DROLET, M.** (1997), "Computers, Fax Machines and Wages in Canada: What really matters?", Unpublished paper, Business and Labour Market Analysis Division, Statistics Canada, Ottawa.

NRC – UNITED STATES NATIONAL RESEARCH COUNCIL (2000), *Building a Workforce for the Information Economy*, National Academy Press, October. http://books.nap.edu/html/IT_workforce/

OECD (1995), "The Measurement of Scientific and Technological Activities: Manual on the measurement of human resources devoted to S&T 'Canberra Manual'", OECD/GD(95)77, Paris.

OECD (1998), *Technology, Productivity and Job Creation: Best policy practices*, Paris.

OECD (1999a), *Employment Outlook*, Paris.

OECD (1999*b*), *OECD Science, Technology and Industry Scoreboard: Benchmarking Knowledge-based Economies*, Paris.

OECD (2000*a*), *A New Economy? The changing role of innovation and information technology in growth*, Paris.

OECD (2000*b*), *Economic Outlook*, Paris.

OECD (2000*c*), *Education at a Glance: OECD Indicators*, CERI, Paris.

OECD (2000*d*), "ICT Skills and Employment, Working party on the information economy", Paris, 15 November, DSTI/ICCP/IE(2000)7.

OECD (2000*e*), *Knowledge Management in the Learning Society*, CERI, Paris.

OECD (2000*f*), "Links between Policy and Growth: Cross-country evidence – Working party No. 1 on macroeconomic and structural policy analysis", ECO/CPE/WP1(2000)12, Paris.

OECD (2000*g*), *Science, Technology and Industry Outlook*, Paris.

OECD (2001), "Knowledge, Work Organisation and Economic Growth", DEELSA/ELSA (2001)2, Paris.

OECD and **STATISTICS CANADA** (2000), *Literacy in the Information Age: Final Report of the International Adult Literacy Survey*, Paris.

OSBERG, L., WOLFF, E. and **BAUMOL, W.** (1989), *The Information Economy: The implications of unbalanced growth*, The Institute for Research on Public Policy, Nova Scotia.

OSTERMAN, P. (1995), "Skill, Training, and Work Organization in American Establishments", *Industrial Relations*, Vol. 34, No. 2.

PONT, B. and **WERQUIN, P.** (2000), "Literacy in a Thousand Words", *OECD Observer*, No. 223, pp. 49-50.

QCA – QUALIFICATIONS AND CURRICULUM AUTHORITY (1997), *Qualifications and Curriculum Authority: An Introduction*, London.

REICH, R. (1991), *The Work of Nations*, Simon and Schuster, New York.

ROSENBAUM, J.E. and **BINDER, A.** (1997), "Do Employers really Need more Educated Youth?", *Sociology of Education*, Vol. 70, January, pp. 68-85.

SANGSTER, D. (1999), "Critical Skills in Five Canadian Industries: A summary report on sectoral interviews", report prepared for the Expert Panel on skills. http://acst-ccst.gc.ca/skills

SHAPIRO, D. and **GOERTZ, M.E.** (1998), "Connecting Work and School: Findings from the National Employers Survey", presented at the annual meeting of the American Education Research Association, April.

STASZ, C. (2000), *Assessing Skills for Work: Two Perspectives*, Oxford Economic Papers.

STASZ, C. and **BREWER, D.J.** (1999), *Academic Skills at Work – Two Perspectives*, reprinted from the National Centre for Research in Vocational Education, RAND Education.

STEEDMAN, H. (1998), "Low Skills: How the supply is changing across Europe", *Trends in the development of occupations and qualifications in Europe*, CEDEFOP, Thessaloniki.

THOMPSON, P., WALLACE, T., FLECKER, G. and **AHLSTRAND, R.** (1995), "It ain't what you do, it's the way that you do it: production organisation and skill utilisation in commercial vehicles", *Work, Employment and Society*, Vol. 9, No. 4, pp. 719-742.

WISE L., CHIA, W.J. and **RUDNER, L.M.** (1990), "Identifying Necessary Job Skills: A review of previous approaches", prepared for the SCANS – The Secretary's Commission on Achieving Necessary Skills, Employment and Training Administration, U.S. Department of Labour.

chapter 5
WHAT FUTURE FOR OUR SCHOOLS?

SUMMARY

What directions will schooling take over the medium to long term, and how might policies shape these futures? These far-reaching questions have inspired the OECD's Centre for Educational Research and Innovation to develop six scenarios for tomorrow's schools.

The first two scenarios project from existing features or trends. Scenario 1 posits the continuation of bureaucratic institutionalised systems, resisting radical change but fulfilling important hidden social functions. Scenario 2 delineates futures where existing market approaches to education are extended much further than today, with both positive and negative results.

Two "re-schooling" scenarios describe a strengthening of schools' public recognition, support and autonomy. In Scenario 3, this comes from schools developing much more powerful social links and community leadership functions. In Scenario 4, most schools have become flexible "learning organisations" with a strong knowledge focus and highly motivated teachers.

Two "de-schooling" futures involve the dismantling of much of school institutions and systems. In Scenario 5, this comes about through the widespread establishment of non-formal learning networks, facilitated both by ICTs and a "network society" environment. In Scenario 6, it comes about through an exodus of teachers that is unresponsive to concerted policy measures and leads to the more or less extensive "meltdown" of school systems.

The chapter concludes with a set of policy questions that arise in relation to all these different futures and options.

There is a need for policy
reflection on the long-term
future of schooling.

1. INTRODUCTION

Schooling is a matter of fundamental importance for the well-being of OECD countries in the broadest terms. Its characteristics and effectiveness are at the heart of education policy. The foregoing chapters in this volume have highlighted the key role of education and learning in fostering skills and competencies and in promoting growth, knowledge, social development and inclusion; schooling plays a central part in furthering these objectives. Equally important, though not necessarily as obvious, schooling has a critical function to perform in the socialisation of the young so that they become healthy individuals and active citizens. This function is, if anything, still more important in a world of rapid change and fragmentation in many other areas of family and community life. It is also during the early years, from early childhood to adolescence, that the bedrock of competence and motivation is laid for a lifetime of learning. Given these critical functions of schooling, policy reflection is needed on future directions over the medium- to long-term as well as on present priorities. This chapter complements the above analyses of on-going developments by just such a long-term discussion.

Forward-looking educational
methodologies remain under-
developed, and scenarios offer
a valuable tool …

The chapter presents six scenarios constructed through the OECD/CERI programme on "Schooling for Tomorrow" (OECD, 2001a). Their purpose is to sharpen understanding of how schooling might develop in the years to come and the potential role of policy to help shape these futures. While this does not exhaust approaches to forward-looking policy thinking, scenario development is a particularly effective way of bringing together the "big picture" of strategic aims, the long-term processes of change, and multiple sets of variables. Perhaps surprisingly, forward thinking of this kind has been relatively little developed in education compared with other policy sectors, despite education's fundamental characteristic of yielding benefits over very long time spans.[1] A major challenge for policy-making in this field is both to make it more genuinely long-term in vision and to integrate more effectively knowledge about education and its wider environment into the process. As the methodologies for educational forward-thinking remain under-developed, there is much to be done in building up a "toolbox" of such approaches to inform the policy-making process. Scenario construction, as presented in this chapter, is one way to do this. It becomes especially effective, however, when undertaken as part of policy formulation in each country. This enables the scenarios to be developed against the concrete trends and realities in place. And, it enables them most effectively to achieve their purpose – to stimulate dialogue between the different stakeholders about change.

2. THE OECD SCHOOLING SCENARIOS

The OECD "Schooling for Tomorrow" scenarios combine different elements – trends, plausible inter-relationships between clusters of variables, and guiding policy ideas. They are thus neither purely empirical (predictions) nor purely

---

1. This point was also emphasised by Ms. Ylva Johansson, the former Swedish Education Minister, in her conclusions as Chair of the November 2000 Rotterdam "Schooling for Tomorrow" conference, in describing forward-thinking approaches as being "woefully under-developed in our field" (Johansson, 2000).

normative (visions). They have been constructed as alternatives for schooling *per se* rather than as educational extrapolations based on scenarios developed for other fields – the social, economic, technological, environmental, cultural, etc. – though, of course, education is strongly influenced by such factors.

Proposing several scenarios underlines that there is not one pathway into the future but many, and they should not be expected to emerge in a "pure" form. Distilling the infinite range of possible futures into a limited number of polar "types", however, stimulates consideration of the strategic choices to be confronted and the principal dimensions of change. The scenarios invite the questions: *a*) how probable, and *b*) how desirable, each is. Having addressed these questions, the task for policy thinking is to consider what might be done to bring the probable and desirable as closely as possible into alignment, making the more desirable futures more likely, and *vice versa*.

... for clarifying what is desirable and what is possible.

The scenarios presented have been constructed in a time frame of approximately 15 to 20 years – long enough for significant change to occur beyond immediate political cycles, but not so far off as to be remote to any but futurists and visionaries. The interest is as much in the intervening processes of change as in the fully-fledged scenarios themselves. The latter may be considered either as stable "steady-states" or as more volatile, and hence likely to set further cycles of change in train.

Six scenarios have been developed through the "Schooling for Tomorrow" programme, refined through a series of events during 2000, ranging from small expert group meetings to larger seminars, and most recently an international conference held in Rotterdam in November. Two of the scenarios are posited on the continued unfolding of existing models ("The status quo extrapolated"), two describe the substantial strengthening of schools with new dynamism, recognition and purpose (described as "Re-schooling"), while the two final scenarios portray future worlds that witness a significant decline in the position of schools ("De-schooling").[2]

Two OECD scenarios extrapolate the status quo, two describe "re-schooling" futures, two "de-schooling".

The "status quo extrapolated"	The "re-schooling" scenarios	The "de-schooling" scenarios
Scenario 1: *Robust Bureaucratic School Systems*	**Scenario 3:** *Schools as Core Social Centres*	**Scenario 5:** *Learner Networks and the Network Society*
Scenario 2: *Extending the Market Model*	**Scenario 4:** *Schools as Focused Learning Organisations*	**Scenario 6:** *Teacher Exodus – the 'Meltdown' Scenario*

2. The sixth "teacher exodus" scenario has been added following workshop discussion during the Rotterdam Conference, in recognition of the fundamental problems that would confront schools in systems where teacher shortages become so seriously exacerbated as to constitute a crisis.

The scenarios are bounded in age terms, covering organised learning from birth up to around completion of secondary education. It is for children and young people of this age range that public responsibility for education is most highly developed in OECD countries, raising a distinct set of policy issues compared with later learning for adults organised through highly diverse arrangements. The six scenarios are not specific to the primary or secondary phases, though it can be expected that certain aspects would apply more directly to one or other of these cycles.

They refer to whole systems, not individual cases.

To facilitate comparison, the scenarios have been constructed within a common framework of clusters of variables that were identified as critical dimensions in determining the shape of school systems: *a*) *Attitudes, expectations, political support*; *b*) *Goals and functions for schooling*; *c*) *Organisation and structures*; *d*) *The geo-political dimension*; *e*) *The teaching force*. Each scenario refers to the systemic "centres of gravity" of schooling arrangements rather than descriptions of particular schools or local cases. While, for instance, there will already be some examples of schools in OECD countries that fit the "re-schooling" features of Scenarios 3 and 4, these would only come about when the large majority of schools can be described as "key social centres" or as "focused learning organisations".

2.1 The "status quo extrapolated"

Scenario 1: "Robust bureaucratic school systems"

- *Strong bureaucracies and robust institutions*

- *Vested interests resist fundamental change*

- *Continuing problems of school image and resourcing*

In Scenario 1, bureaucratic systems remain strong and resist radical change ...

This scenario is built on the continuation of dominant school systems, characterised by strong bureaucratic elements and pressures towards uniformity. Despite education being to the fore on political agendas, robust schools and systems prove to be extremely resistant to radical change, because of the strength of the vested interests of the powerful stakeholders. Resource levels do not pass the thresholds that would allow longstanding criticisms of schools to be laid to rest or quality to be generally assured. New tasks and responsibilities are continually added to the remit of schools, in the face of the problems arising within the other core socialisation settings of family and community, causing schools' financial and human resources to be continually stretched. The norms of completed years spent by students in schools and initial education continues to go up, and the diplomas so gained are widely regarded as the main passports to the next stages of life (though in reality the links are more complex). Despite repeated policy initiatives, the educational inequalities that reflect unequal social and residential home backgrounds/environments prove extremely resilient (see Chapter 3 of this volume).

Scenario 1

Education, especially schooling, is politicised, and to the fore in party politics. Despite continued grumbling about the state of schools from parents, employers and the media, most are basically opposed to radical change. More positive attitudes held towards local than overall provision. Possibilities for "playing the system" are important in ensuring the continued support of schools by educated parents resulting in pressure for the greater exercise of choice.	*Attitudes, expectations, political support*
Much attention focuses on the curriculum, with many countries operating a common curriculum and assessment system – aimed at enforcing standards or creating greater formal equality or both. Formal certificates are seen as main passports to economic/ social life – but while increasingly necessary they are increasingly insufficient. Larger relative numbers and greater diversity of "older young" in initial education as the norm continues of staying on longer and longer. Continuing inequalities alongside policy endeavours to combat failure	*Goals and functions*
Strong bureaucratic character of schools and systems continues. Dominance of the classroom/individual teacher model, but some room for innovation and for developing schools as learning organisations. Increased ICT use in schools but not radical change to organisational structures of teaching and learning. Growing but patchy connections between educational and "non-educational" community uses of school facilities.	*Organisations and structures*
The nation (or state/province in federal systems) is still the main locus of political authority but squeezed by: – decentralisation to schools and communities… – new corporate and media interests in the learning market and … – globalising pressures, including growing use of international surveys of educational performance.	*The geo-political dimension*
Highly distinct teacher corps, sometimes with civil service status. Strong unions and associations in many countries and centralised industrial relations. Professional status and rewards are problematic in most countries. "Craft" models of professionalism remain strong. Growing attention to professional development (INSET), and efforts to retain teachers. This is partly in the face of major teacher supply problems, exacerbated by ageing.	*The teaching force*

*... while performing
fundamental tasks that are
not always well recognised.*

While schools are continually criticised for being out-dated and slow to change – accusations such as being excessively bureaucratic, with teachers wedded to traditional instruction methods – some inertia may simply be inherent in the nature of school systems. It may only be expected in societies that expect a great deal from schools, seeking to include all young people for ever-longer time periods with ever-fuller curricula, while being unwilling to invest on the very large scale that might bring about fundamental, as opposed to incremental, change. Societies, including parents, may well prefer only gradual evolution in their schools. This scenario also recognises that schools perform many fundamental tasks (looking after children, providing protected space for interaction and play, socialisation, sorting and selection) that generally pass unnoticed compared with the obvious ones of imparting literacy, numeracy, disciplinary knowledge, and diplomas (Hutmacher, 1999). The question then is: "If schools systems were not in place for these purposes, what alternatives would serve them better?" Fragmentation in families and communities, the other settings in which children are socialised, reinforces the pertinence of this question (see Scenario 3).

The OECD's Rotterdam Conference acknowledged the many successes of school systems, despite their imperfections: "In sum", said its chair, Ylva Johansson in her conclusions, "schools have been very important and, in many respects, successful institutions. They were integral to the transformation from agrarian to industrial societies. They represent a very important invest-ment for our countries in making the further transformation from industrial to the knowledge-based societies of today and tomorrow, but for this they must be revitalised and dynamic" (Johansson, 2000). The final condition – the need for revitalisation – is, however, a critical caveat to her perception of schools' continued effectiveness into the future.

*New forces – such as ICTs or
teacher crisis – may still
break open the "status quo".*

Yet, even if school systems are excessively bureaucratic and slow to create such dynamism themselves, there may now be developments in train that will force disruption to the *status quo*. Among the most important of these factors are the growing power of learners and parents as "consumers"; the impact of ICTs in eroding established school and classroom boundaries; and a potential crisis of teacher supply. (These factors are reflected in the scenarios outlined below, including "extending the market model", "learner networks and the network society", and "teacher exodus – the 'meltdown' scenario".) It remains to be seen whether schools can accommodate such pressures, as they have many times before, or whether there will be major ruptures with the past.

Scenario 2: "Extending the market model"

- *Widespread dissatisfaction leads to re-shaping public funding and school systems*

- *Rapid growth of demand-driven "market currencies", indicators and accreditation*

- *Greater diversity of providers and professionals, greater inequality*

Trends towards more market-oriented schooling models – of organisation, delivery and management – are much closer to the experience and cultures of some countries than others. In this scenario, these trends are extended significantly in the face of widespread dissatisfaction with the performance of relatively uniform structures of public school systems and with existing funding arrangements to provide cost-effective solutions. In response to these pressures, governments encourage diversification and the emergence of new learning providers through funding structures, incentives and de-regulation, and discover considerable market potential, nationally and internationally. Significant injections of private household and corporate finance are stimulated.

In Scenario 2, market approaches to schooling expand significantly...

New market "currencies" of indicators, measures, and accreditation of both learners and providers flourish, while direct public monitoring and curriculum regulation decline. Public education, schools and the government role do not disappear, despite greater privatisation and more mixed public/private partnerships, though outcomes depend greatly on the funding and regulation regimes being introduced and may differ significantly between the primary and secondary levels. In an atmosphere of shake-up, innovation and imaginative solutions abound as do painful experiences of the transitions. Alongside the positive features of fresh thinking are the seriously enhanced risks of inequality and exclusion and of the public school system being relegated to "residual" status.

... stimulating widespread innovation, but creating difficult transitions and widening inequalities.

The development of a much more market-oriented model for schooling is likely to depend on a number of factors. It would be fuelled by a substantial sense of dissatisfaction with established provision among "strategic consumers", especially articulate middle-class parents and political parties, combined with a culture where schooling is already viewed as much as a private as a public good. Wide differences of educational performance would add weight to the criticisms, while the significant development of the "market model" in schooling would itself be supported by a degree of social tolerance of inequality. The nature of the teaching force could be a determining factor. A crisis of teacher supply (see Scenario 6) might well quicken the search for market-based models as it would for other alternatives. And, while a fragmented teaching force might be conducive to such changes through its impotence to prevent them, a monolithic profession resisting innovation could conceivably produce the same result.

Dissatisfaction by "strategic consumers" provides impetus for market solutions...

The business environment is likely to be highly influential, but in which direction is not necessarily clear-cut. On the one hand, more aggressive entrepreneurial cultures might be best for identifying new markets and approaches that break with convention. On the other, highly developed traditions of human resource development, with a deep understanding of "soft skills" and learning, might be needed to generate successful demand-oriented approaches of competence development, measurement and accreditation. Political tradition and government action would clearly be critical – in setting market terms, encouraging alternative forms of supply, permitting the exercise of demand. Its role would also be important in managing what could be a painful set of transition processes. Such responsibilities notwithstanding, this scenario assumes a diminished direct government role in provision.

... but while entrepreneurial and political cultures influence schooling, in which direction is not clear-cut.

Scenario 2

Attitudes, expectations, political support	Significantly reduced belief in the value of public education overall. Possible funding "revolts" by taxpayers.
	Divergent and conflicting positions expressed. Teachers associations unable to resist moves to greater privatisation.
	A political culture develops that supports extended competition across many areas of social, employment, and cultural policy.
	The stability of new market solutions highly dependent on how well they meet perceived shortcomings.
Goals and functions	Different indicators and accreditation arrangements become basic to market operations; "efficiency" and "quality" are prominent criteria. Decline of established curriculum structures defined in terms of programmes and delivery, re-defined as outcomes.
	Alongside the strong focus on knowledge and skills, values and attitudes – such as attitudes to risk, co-operation and hard work – may be prominent and hence recognised as outcomes. Market-oriented schooling may also, in response to demand, allow greater reflection of cultural/religious beliefs.
	Stronger emphasis on information, guidance and marketing – some publicly organised, much private.
	Substantial tolerance of inequalities and exclusion. Possible tendency for greater homogeneity of learner groups.
	Lifelong learning becomes the norm for many. Clear boundaries for "staying on" in school lose meaning in the face of diversified educational careers.
Organisations and structures	Privatisation, public/private partnerships, voucher systems, and diverse management are the norm. Individualisation and home schooling flourish. Greater experimentation with organisational forms. Many existing programmes disappear.
	Possible big differences emerge between the primary and secondary sectors, with market models more strongly developed at secondary level.
	Markets develop in childcare and culture, not just in employment-related learning.
	ICTs are much more extensively and imaginatively exploited for learning. Networking flourishes where tangible gains perceived by all parties; otherwise competition inhibits co-operation. Copyright issues acute.
The geo-political dimension	Substantially reduced role for central providers and public education authorities. They still oversee market regulation, but much less traditional "steering" and "monitoring".
	International providers and accreditation agencies become more powerful, but strong players, many private, operate at each level – local, national, international.
	Much more diverse set of stake-holders involved in educational governance.
	Funding arrangements, including absolute levels of resources, are critical in shaping new learning markets.

Less distinct teaching force and a wide range of new professionals with diverse profiles – public, private; full-time, part-time. Potential quality issues.

The new "teaching professionals" in ready supply in areas of residential desirability and/or learning market opportunity. Otherwise, problems of shortages and speed of market adjustment.

Flourishing training and accreditation for professionals to operate in the learning market.

Transition problems until new markets become embedded.

There is substantial interest in market approaches in some countries and quarters and many pertinent developments (hence this scenario is included in "The status quo extrapolated"). But, they cover a bewildering variety: the enhanced exercise of parental choice, including in some cases through vouchers; the involvement of the private sector in the running of schools or parts of systems; substantial household contributions for supplementary private tuition as in Japan or Korea, or for attendance at private schools (such as the oddly-named English "Public schools"); the public funding of "private" institutions organised by particular cultural, religious or citizen groups; the corporate promotion of the e-learning market, and others. The recent UNESCO *Courier* ("Education: the Last Frontier for Profit", November 2000) magazine is but one expression of interest in new market approaches. The title conveys well an underlying ambiguity: is education a frontier on the point of being breached by the profit motive or is it so distinct that it will continue to resist? Much might turn on the *level* of education in question. Flourishing corporate initiatives in the ICT learning market at tertiary level, for example, stand in contrast with modest growth in schools. The further question then is about where the main boundaries will be drawn in the applicability of this scenario – between secondary and tertiary (in which case it would not be a schooling scenario as such)? Between lower and upper secondary? Between primary and lower secondary?

Many market examples exist, but how far should they be extended in schooling?

2.2 The "re-schooling" scenarios

Scenario 3: "Schools as core social centres"

- *High levels of public trust and funding*
- *Schools as centres of community and social capital formation*
- *Greater organisational/professional diversity, greater social equity*

In this scenario, the school comes to enjoy widespread recognition as the most effective bulwark against social fragmentation and a crisis of values. There is a strong sense of schooling as a "public good" and a marked upward shift in the general status and level of support for schools. The individualisation of learning

In Scenario 3, schools as high status, community institutions provide a bulwark against fragmentation.

is tempered by a clear collective emphasis. Greater priority is accorded to the social/community role of schools, with more explicit sharing of programmes and responsibilities with the other settings of further and continuing education/training. Poor areas in particular enjoy high levels of support (financial, teaching, expertise and other community-based resources).

Greater resource equality, experimentation, school autonomy and shared roles....

Overall, schools concentrate more on laying the cognitive and non-cognitive foundations of knowledge, skills, attitudes and values for students to be built on thereafter as part of lifelong learning. Norms of lengthening duration in initial schooling may well be reversed, and there is greater experimentation with age/grading structures and the involvement of learners of all ages. Schools come to enjoy a large measure of autonomy without countervailing central constraints, as levels of public/political support and funding have been attained through a widespread perception of high standards, evenly distributed, thereby reducing the felt need closely to monitor conformity to established standards. Strong pressures for corrective action nevertheless come into play in the face of evidence that any particular school is under-performing. There is more active sharing of professional roles between the core of teachers and other sources of experience and expertise, including different interest, religious, and community groups.

Scenario 3

Attitudes, expectations, political support

Wide measure of party political and public agreement on goals and the value of public education; funding increases.

High-trust politics with extensive co-operation between authorities, teachers, employers, and other community groups in relation to schools.

The role of schools as centres of community activity/identity is accorded widespread recognition.

Educated classes and media supportive of schools, giving them greater freedom to develop their own pathways as centres of social solidarity/capital in different partnerships.

Goals and functions

The role of schools continues in transmitting, legitimising and accrediting knowledge, but with greater recognition and focus on a range of other social and cultural outcomes, including citizenship.

More diverse forms of competence recognition developed in enterprises and the labour market liberate schools from excessive pressures of credentialism.

The lifelong learning function more explicit. Possible reversal of trend to longer school careers, but less clear-cut boundaries between school participation and non-participation.

Inequalities reduced but diversity widens and social cohesion strengthened.

Strong distinct schools reinvigorated by new organisational forms, less bureaucratic, more diverse.

Organisations and structures

General erosion of "high school walls". Wide diversity of student body, greater inter-generational mixing and joint youth-adult activities.

Sharp divisions between primary and secondary levels are softened; possible re-emergence of all-age schools.

ICTs are strongly developed, with particular emphasis on communication (by students, teachers, parents, community, other stakeholders). Networking flourishes.

The local dimension of schooling substantially boosted, supported by strong national frameworks, particularly in support of communities with weak social infrastructure.

The geo-political dimension

New forms of governance are developed giving various groups, enterprises, etc, a bigger role.

International awareness and exchange is strong, but supra-national control is not, encouraging local diversity.

A core of high-status teaching professionals, but not necessarily in lifetime careers.

The teaching force

More varied contractual arrangements and conditions, but significant increases of rewards for all.

A prominent role for other professionals, community actors, parents, etc. More complex combinations of teaching with other community responsibilities.

This scenario describes a strengthened, creative school institution available to all communities, meeting critical social responsibilities while silencing critics. This scenario fits a longstanding tradition advocating that closer links be forged between schools and local communities. More recently, such arguments have acquired an added urgency and relevance with the fragmentation occurring in many family and community settings, raising new concerns about the socialisation of children. In response to these concerns, the school could thus become a much-needed "social anchor" (Kennedy, 2001) and constitute the fulcrum of residential communities (Carnoy, 2001). Some analyses suggest that "social capital" may be in a process of erosion in a number of OECD countries to the detriment of individual well-being, society and the economy (OECD, 2001b).[3] In this scenario, the school is instrumental in arresting this trend, benefiting in the process from the positive impact on educational achievement of strengthened infrastructure and belief in the values upheld by schools.

… help schools contribute to the development of social capital.

This future for the place called school would call for very major changes in most countries – more than would normally be feasible even over a 15-to-20-year time period. The scenario is predicated not only on important re-definitions of

The scenario's demanding prerequisites may be unrealistic.

---

3. Though the empirical evidence on declining social capital remains mixed and as yet inconclusive; see also Putnam (2000).

purpose, practice and professionalism, but also on the new definitions being widely endorsed by the main stakeholders throughout society. Generous resourcing would probably be called for, given the need for very even patterns of quality learning environments across all communities and for establishing high esteem for teachers and schools, though some of this might be attained through more cost-effective resource use. Greater flexibility of action would also be needed. If schools could rely on the existence of universal opportunities for continuing education and the certification of competencies outside education, this would be a major step in liberating them from the excessive burdens of credentialism; in these circumstances such flexibility might well be more attainable. However desirable any of these prerequisites to this scenario may be, they are not necessarily very likely in the foreseeable future.

Closer ties to communities may widen not narrow inequalities.

Furthermore, the problems relating to communities and social capital that make this scenario attractive could equally be the very factors that prevent it being fully realised. Far from equalising the effect of different socio-economic environments, the strategy of linking schools very closely with their communities might only serve to exacerbate the gaps between the vibrant and the depressed. Hence, without powerful mechanisms equalising resources and status, and without a strong sense of common purpose, the risk is that scenario would reflect, even exacerbate, existing inequalities between different communities [discussed in relation to "educational priority zones" (ZEPs) by Michel, 2001]. These problems would need to be overcome if the future is to lie with this radical form of "re-schooling".

Scenario 4: " Schools as focused learning organisations"

- *High levels of public trust and funding*
- *Schools and teachers network widely in learning organisations*
- *Strong quality and equity features*

In Scenario 4, most schools are "learning organisations" with strong knowledge focus...

In this scenario, schools are revitalised around a strong "knowledge" agenda, with far-reaching implications for the organisation of individual institutions and for the system as a whole. The academic/artistic/competence development goals are paramount; experimentation and innovation are the norm. Curriculum specialisms flourish as do innovative forms of assessment and skills recognition. As with the previous scenario, all this takes place in a high-trust environment where quality norms rather than accountability measures are the primary means of control. Similarly, generous resourcing would probably be required, though there would be very close attention to how those resources are used in pursuit of quality. Professionals (teachers and other specialists) would in general be highly motivated, learning groups are small, and they work in environments characterised by the continuing professional development of personnel, group activities, and networking. In these environments, a strong emphasis is placed on educational R&D. ICTs are used extensively alongside other learning media, traditional and new.

In this scenario, the very large majority of schools merit the label "learning organisations". They are among the lead organisations driving the "lifelong learning for all" agenda, informed by a strong equity ethos (thereby distinguishing Scenario 4 from the two "status quo" scenarios in which quality learning is distributed much more unevenly). Close links develop between schools, places of tertiary education, media companies and other enterprises, individually and collectively.

... and they are afforded high levels of support, trust and flexibility, and advance equity aims.

Scenario 4

Wide measure of party political agreement on goals and on the value of education as a "public good".

Attitudes, expectations, political support

Very high levels of public support for schools, including through funding where this is judged necessary. Care taken to ensure the gaps between more and less endowed schools do not widen learning opportunities.

Educated classes and the media are supportive of schools, permitting an environment of freedom to individualise their programmes. High-trust politics.

Schools work hard to maintain their supportive constituency and generally succeed in lowering "school walls".

Highly demanding curricula are the norm for all students. More specialisms catered for (arts, technology, languages, etc.) but a demanding mix of learning expected of all students, including specialists.

Goals and functions

School diplomas continue to enjoy major currency, albeit alongside other forms of competence recognition. Innovative developments of assessment, certification and skills recognition for broad sets of talents.

The lifelong learning function is made more explicit through clarification and implementation of the foundation role for lifelong learning. Extensive guidance and counselling arrangements.

A major investment made in equality of high quality opportunities – overt failure considerably reduced by high expectations, the targeting of poor communities, and eradication of low quality programmes.

Strong schools as learning organisations with distinct profiles. Flatter, team-oriented organisations with greater attention to management skills for all personnel.

Organisations and structures

Team approaches are the norm. Intense attention to new knowledge about the processes of teaching and learning, and the production, mediation and use of knowledge in general. Major new investments in R&D.

Wide variety in age, grading and ability mixes, with more all-age and school/ tertiary combinations.

ICTs are strongly developed, both as a tool for learning and analysis and for communication.

Links between schools, tertiary education, and "knowledge industries" are commonplace – for INSET, research and consultancy.

The geo-political dimension	Strong national framework and support, with particular focus on communities with weakest social resources.
	International networking of students and teachers.
	Countries moving furthest towards this scenario attract considerable international attention as "world leaders".
	Substantial involvement of multi-national as well as national companies in schools (but close attention given to widening gaps).
The teaching force	A high status teaching corps, enjoying good rewards and conditions.
	Somewhat fewer in lifetime careers, with greater mobility in and out of teaching and other professions.
	More varied contractual arrangements but good rewards for all.
	Major increase in staffing levels, allowing greater innovation in teaching and learning, professional development, and research.
	Networking is the norm among teachers, and between them and other sources of expertise.

This differs from the previous scenario by its stronger "knowledge" focus that is well understood by the public and avoids the risk of ever-widening social remits making impossible demands on schools. It assumes strong schools, enjoying very high levels of public support and generous funding from diverse sources, as well as a large degree of latitude to develop programmes and methods. The teacher corps remains a more distinct profession, albeit with mobility and using various sources of expertise, than in the "school as social centre" scenario.

But Scenario 4 is not typical of today's practice, and its conditions are hard to create. Many in education would regard this "learning organisation" scenario as highly desirable but at least two related sets of problems stand in the way of transforming the desirable into the probable. First, OECD analysis has shown that this model is very far from typical of practice in schools across different countries (OECD, 2000*b*). The scenario would thus call for radical breaks with established practice especially by and among teachers that, as discussed in relation to Scenario 1, could be extremely difficult to realise on a broad scale. Second, as with the previous scenario, the formulation begs questions of how to create a very supportive media and political educational environment, ensure such generous funding levels, and capture high status for schools and teachers where these do not already exist. Such conditions are far from being met in most countries at present, implying concerted strategies and investments to turn this situation around. Similarly, this scenario's equality assumptions are highly demanding, yet the analysis in Chapter 3 of this volume shows just how entrenched learning inequalities remain. In short, this scenario remains a good way off, whatever the progress in particular schools and pockets of excellence.

2.3 The "de-schooling" scenarios

Scenario 5: "Learner networks and the network society"

- *Widespread dissatisfaction with/rejection of organised school systems*
- *Non-formal learning using ICT potential reflects the "network society"*
- *Communities of interest, potentially serious equity problems*

Whether schools are criticised for being too reflective of unequal social and economic structures, or insufficiently reflective of diverse cultures, or out of tune with economic life, in this scenario these very different sources of criticisms take firm root. Dissatisfaction with available provision leads to a quickening abandonment of school institutions through diverse alternatives in a political environment supportive of the need for change. This is further stimulated by the extensive possibilities opened up by the Internet and continually developing forms of powerful and inexpensive ICTs (see OECD, 1999). The result is the radical de-institutionalisation, even dismantling, of school systems.

In Scenario 5, institutions and systems are dismantled…

What takes their place is part of the emerging "network society". Learning for the young is not primarily conferred in particular places called "schools" nor through professionals called "teachers" nor necessarily located in distinct residential community bases. Much more diverse cultural, religious and community voices come to be reflected in the day-to-day socialisation and learning arrangements for children in the "network society". Some are very local in character, but there are also extensive opportunities for distance and cross-border learning and networking. The demarcations between the initial and continuing phases of lifelong learning come to be substantially blurred. While these arrangements are supported as promoting diversity and democracy, they may also bring substantial risks of exclusion especially for those students who have traditionally relied on the school as the mechanism for social mobility and inclusion.

… and are replaced by diverse learning networks as part of the "Network Society".

Scenario 5

Widespread dissatisfaction with the institution called "school" – its bureaucratic nature and perceived inability to deliver learning tailored to complex, diverse societies.

Attitudes, expectations, political support

Flight out of schools by the educated classes as well as other community, interest and religious groups, supported by political parties, media, multimedia companies in the learning market.

New forms of private, voluntaristic and community funding arrangements emerge in tune with general developments towards the "network society".

Goals and functions	The decline of established curriculum structures with the dismantling of the school system. Key role for different values and attitudes.
	New attention comes to be given to "childcare" arrangements with the demise of schools. Some of these are based on sports and other cultural community activities.
	Hard to predict how far various measures of competence become the driving "currency". To the extent that they do, strong emphasis on information, guidance and marketing through ICTs, and on new forms of accreditation of competence.
	Possibly wide inequalities open up between those participating in the network society and those who do not.
Organisations and structures	Much learning would take place on an individualised basis, or through networks of learners, parents and professionals.
	ICTs much more extensively exploited for learning and networking, with flourishing software market.
	If some schools do survive, hard to predict whether these would be mainly at the primary level (focused on basic knowledge and socialisation) or at secondary level (focused on advanced knowledge and labour market entry).
	Some public schools remain for those otherwise excluded by the "digital divide" or community-based networks – either very well-resourced institutions or else "sink" schools.
The geo-political dimension	Community players and aggressive media companies are among those helping to "disestablish" schools in national systems. Local and international dimensions strengthened at expense of the national.
	While international measurements and accountability less relevant as systems and schools break up, new forms of international accreditation might emerge for elites.
	Bridging the "digital divide" and market regulation become major roles for the public authorities, as well as overseeing the remaining publicly-provided school sector.
	Groups of employers may become very active if these arrangements do not deliver an adequate skills base and if government is unwilling to re-establish schools.
The teaching force	Demarcations between teacher and student, parent and teacher, education and community, blur and break down. Networks bring different clusters together according to perceived needs.
	New learning professionals emerge, employed especially by the major players in the network market. These operate via surgeries, various forms of "helpline" and home visits.

Scenarios based around these ideas are among the most commonly proposed as "visions" for the future of schooling. They have the appeal of offering, for those in search of change, a clear alternative to the more school-based models outlined above. The scenario can be understood as a feature of already-visible developments towards the "network society" (Castells, 1996), building on the potential of ICTs to provide the means for learning and networking beyond time and place constraints. It is in tune with those messages of the broader lifelong learning agenda stressing flexibility, individualisation, and the role of non-formal learning. In relation to school-age learning, home schooling is growing and some predict this will quicken into the future, even if it is still relatively small-scale in most countries (Hargreaves, 1999). While sharing some common features with the "market model" of Scenario 2, the driving force in this scenario is co-operation rather than competition, again appealing to those in search of alternative "post-industrial" paradigms.

These ideas are common among futurists as a clear alternative to school-based approaches.

Yet, it also raises serious questions of feasibility and sustainability. How well would such arrangements meet the range of critical "hidden" functions, including of socialisation, that has made the school such a universal model and so resilient (as discussed under Scenario 1)? What would happen to those individuals and communities who are not active participants in the "network society" and who have low social capital? It is possible that this scenario would actually deepen the "digital divide" (OECD, 2000a). This scenario, therefore, also runs into potentially severe inequality problems, raising the prospect of government intervention in ways that would undermine the very distinctiveness of this scenario. Does it really provide a feasible scenario for the 21st century or is it instead proposing a return to 18th/19th century educational arrangements (plus the Internet)? Along with such questions about feasibility are those to do with stability/volatility – does it describe a "steady-state" future or a transition point calling for further transformation?

But, is this scenario feasible or sustainable?

Scenario 6: "Teacher exodus – The 'meltdown scenario'"

- *Severe teacher shortages do not respond to policy action*
- *Retrenchment, conflict, and falling standards leading to areas of "meltdown", or*
- *Crisis provides spur to widespread innovation but future still uncertain*

This scenario can be regarded as an elaboration of a "worst case" in response to the question posed in conclusion of Scenario 1 – would the "status quo" survive were teacher shortages to turn into a real staffing crisis? This "meltdown scenario" comes about through the conjuncture of four main factors: *a*) a highly skewed teacher age profile resulting in outflows through retirement far out-stripping inflows of new recruits; *b*) a long period with very tight labour market conditions and general skill shortages resulting in severe difficulties both to recruit new teachers and to retain them in the profession; *c*) the upward shift in teacher rewards and/or staffing levels needed to make a tangible impact on relative attractiveness being viewed as prohibitively expensive, given the sheer numbers involved; and *d*) even when measures

Teacher supply problems reach crisis proportions threatening "meltdown" ...

are proving effective, they require long delays before a noticeable effect results in greater numbers of practising teachers, making it still harder to break into the vicious circles.

The scenario posits a staffing crisis in a context that differs in at least two important respects from that of the "baby boom" of the 1960s. First, the quality demands and expectations of students for extended educational careers have moved on substantially in forty years. Second, the attractiveness of school-level teaching as a career has declined against a continuing upward trend in the share of advanced-skill posts throughout the economy as a whole, posts that often enjoy greater rewards. This combination of factors comes together in this scenario in the form of a very serious crisis for schools, rather than assuming that the problems will always be "muddled through".

As the teacher exodus takes hold and the scale of the "meltdown" crisis is recognised, potentially very different outcomes could be part of Scenario 6. At one extreme, a vicious circle of retrenchment, conflict, and decline sets in, exacerbating the inequalities and problems further. At the other, the teacher crisis provides the spur to radical innovation and change, with different stakeholders joining forces behind far-reaching emergency strategies. Even in that more optimistic case, "meltdown" would not necessarily be avoided. In between, a more evolutionary response to the crisis might be that rewards and attractiveness of the profession increase leading eventually to reconstruction. Whether actions taken would allow another scenario to take the place of "meltdown" would depend critically on the room for manoeuvre permitted by social and political cultures.

Scenario 6

Attitudes, expectations, political support	Widespread public and media dissatisfaction with the state of education in the face of the teacher recruitment crisis and growing sense of declining standards, especially in worst-affected areas.
	Relative political impotence to address the loss from the teaching force given the scale and long-term nature of the problem and/or deep-seated cultural barriers to changes needed to set in train another of the scenarios.
	The education political climate becomes either increasingly conflictual or leads to consensual emergency strategies.
Goals and functions	Established curriculum structures are under intense pressure, especially in shortage subjects. Where main response is one of retrenchment, examinations and accountability mechanisms are strengthened in a bid to halt sliding standards.
	Where the teacher shortage instead stimulates widespread change, major revisions of curricula are undertaken – much more outcome- and demand-oriented and less supply- and programme-centred. New forms of parallel evaluation and assessment methods are developed.
	Inequalities widen sharply between residential areas, social and cultural groups, etc. Affluent parents in worst-affected areas desert public education in favour of private alternatives.

Organisations and structures

Very diverse organisational responses to lack of teachers. In some situations, there is a return to highly traditional methods, partly through public pressure in response to declining standards, partly because of large classes.

In other situations, innovative organisational responses using different forms of expertise (including from tertiary education, enterprises, communities), and diverse mixes of lectures, student groupings, home learning, ICTs, etc.

Intensive use of ICTs as an alternative to teachers; ICT companies are very actively involved. Wide disparities are again possible between highly innovative and traditional uses.

The geo-political dimension

The position of the national authorities is strengthened in the face of crisis, as they acquire extended powers. It weakens, however, the longer the crises are unresolved.

Communities with no serious teacher shortages seek to protect themselves and extend their autonomy from national authorities.

Corporate and media interests in the learning market intensify.

International solidarity improves between some countries where initiatives develop to "lend" and "borrow" trained teachers, including between North and South.

Solidarity declines and protectionist responses increase the more generalised the shortages and where several countries are competing for limited pools of qualified staff.

The teaching force

Teacher rewards increase as part of measures to tackle shortages.

Conditions of teaching worsen as numbers fall, with problems acute in worst-affected areas, exacerbating the sense of crisis.

Strenuous efforts made to bring trained – especially retired – teachers back into schools. Often only disappointing results, particularly where school politics very conflictual and in areas of severe shortage.

In some countries, the distinctiveness of the teacher corps and role of unions/associations increase in proportion to their relative scarcity. In others, established conventions, contractual arrangements, and career structures are rapidly eroded.

As schools shorten teaching time, many posts are created for semi-professional "child-minding." The market in home tuition flourishes, possibly with government subsidies to lower-income households.

Signs of problems in teacher supply are apparent …

Is this scenario likely? As yet the requisite studies are unavailable, but there are some indications that this scenario might be plausible. OECD countries have moved rapidly from being "industrial" to "post-industrial" societies: two-thirds are in service employment across the OECD, approaching three quarters of all jobs in a number of countries, compared with between a half and a quarter or even less at mid-20th century (OECD, 1994, Table 1.2 and OECD, 2000*d*). The job market in which teachers are being recruited and employed is shifting markedly, including the continuing growth of demand for advanced skills as charted in the previous chapter. Teacher salaries, standing, and conditions, in the different combinations that shape a profession's "attractiveness", struggle to compete with the wide range of professional alternatives now available.

... but unevenly distributed, between and within countries.

Most importantly, perhaps, the profession is ageing in many countries, in some cases rapidly. European statistics (European Commission, Eurydice, Eurostat, 2000) suggest that more than a fifth of practising teachers are within a decade of retirement in the majority of EU countries, rising to above a third in Italy which has the highest EU level. There are even higher percentages in the Central European "pre-accession" countries, where as many as 40% are counted in this 10-year pre-retirement phase in the Czech Republic. A third of primary teachers were aged 50 years and over in 1996/97 in Germany and Sweden, as are a quarter in Finland and Italy. Among secondary teachers, over 30% fall in this 50+ age band in these four countries, up to as high as 50% in Sweden (published OECD teacher data are incomplete, but the 2001 edition of *Education at a Glance* will carry a special focus on teachers). While conditions do and will vary widely from one country to another, this area deserves closer international study, including approaches that promise to enhance teacher supply.

3. CONCLUSIONS

As stated at the outset of this chapter, these scenarios have been developed in order to clarify the main directions and strategic options for schooling over the long-term, as well as the policy issues that arise in shaping different futures. They are tools for reflection, not analytical predictions. In the first scenario, large, bureaucratic systems continue as the norm, through the strength of the interests with a major stake in them and through the sheer difficulty of organising equally effective alternatives. In the second, market approaches are extended much more radically, bringing innovation and dynamism but also augmented risks of exclusion. In the third, schools are strengthened significantly by investing in them as focal centres for communities, giving them a range of important new tasks, responsibilities and partners. The fourth sees "learning organisations" for the young become typical of the very large majority of schools, based on demanding, flexible programmes for all. The fifth scenario presents schooling consistent with a highly developed "network society", heavily exploiting ICT's potential and leading to the widespread dismantling of school institutions. The final scenario addresses a future in which teacher shortages reach crisis levels and yet prove largely resistant to the policy initiatives taken to rectify them.

Policy options can be developed in terms of strategic challenges and deliverable goals.

Policy issues have been raised in the discussion of each scenario. Professor Michael Barber, in the Keynote Address to the Rotterdam Conference (2000), suggested a framework through which policy options can be developed in each country in terms of "strategic challenges" and "deliverable goals".[4] This concluding section poses a number of the questions that arise from the alternative scenarios that can usefully be addressed in delineating the policy challenges and the goals to be pursued.

The cultural and political environment. Public attitudes, the degree of consensus or conflict over goals, (dis)satisfaction with schools, and the level of recognition and esteem in which they and teachers are held, will all be critical in shaping the future of schooling. The broad environment becomes even more critical the more that schools are called upon to be autonomous, work in partnerships, and orient themselves to demand. Should this environment be viewed largely as a given and beyond the reach of educational policy? Or instead, should it be treated as an important target of policy strategies, with a view to setting in train virtuous circles on matters that are beyond the reach of regulation and administration?

Can the cultural and political environment be a variable of educational policy?

Accountability. This is an integral feature of all the scenarios, though Scenario 5 – learner networks and the network society – assumes a much-reduced degree of control. The mechanisms through which accountability is realised, however, differ widely across the scenarios: from those based on the close monitoring of performance and attainments, to the accountability generated by the exercise of "client demand", to that exerted by widely-shared norms of demanding quality standards. As demands on schools grow, and with it the costs of failure, how can the need for accountability be assured without its mechanisms undermining the very quality and flexibility they are intended to promote?

How can accountability be assured without undermining flexibility of action?

Diversity vs. uniformity. One of the strengths of the systemic "status quo" model is its pursuit of a formally equal opportunity structure, even if this may come with excessive bureaucracy, and, as shown in Chapter 3, continuing actual inequalities. In the other scenarios (except Scenario 6), major departures from standardisation are sought, though by different routes and approaches to inclusion/exclusion. Important equity questions are raised by all the scenarios. Can schools pursue much more diversified pathways without stumbling over powerful accountability pressures to standardise? Under what conditions does democratic diversity become unacceptable inequality? How far can schooling, which reflects communities and the broader society, be expected to attain much more equal and equitable outcomes, and up to what price are societies willing to pay to do so?

There is a need for greater diversity, but what are the risks of widening inequality?

Resourcing. Schooling requires numerous resources – finance, professional expertise, technical infrastructure and facilities, community and parental support. Outcomes depend not only on their levels, but on their nature and how they are used, managed, and combined. Hence, there are not clear resource implications attached to the scenarios, though broad possibilities

Sufficient resources will need to be marshalled to meet high ambitions – how will they be found?

---

4. He proposed five "strategic challenges" – Reconceptualising Teaching; Creating High Autonomy/High Performance; Building Capacity and Managing Knowledge; Establishing New Partnerships; and Reinventing the Role of Government – and four "deliverable goals" to meet these challenges: Achieving Universally High Standards; Narrowing the Achievement Gap; Unlocking Individualisation; and Promoting Education with Character.

are suggested. Certain of them – Scenarios 2, 3, and 5 particularly – are consistent with diversification of the resource base, with or without a major change in educational spending in relation to GDP. Scenarios 3, 4 and 6 may well call for significant increases in the total spending effort. Scenarios 2 and 5 in particular could well see widening inequalities in resources per student. Whichever scenario unfolds in the future, fundamental resource questions will arise. Are societies willing to invest sufficiently in schools for the tasks being expected of them? If resources are stretched too far to sustain high-quality learning environments and if it is unrealistic to expect major new resource inputs, where might they be found through redistribution, especially in a lifelong learning framework? Is there room for major increases in resource effectiveness in schools and, if so, how?

New demanding models of professionalism – but how to recruit enough teachers?

Teachers. The human resources – the professionals working in schools – are clearly fundamental to the future. Teachers become still more critical to the success of schooling as expectations about quality increase – more demand-oriented approaches and less supply-determined; more active and less passive learning; knowledge creation not just transmission in schools. Responses to these pressures will often result in teachers having to operate in new organisational structures, in close collaboration with colleagues and through networks, facilitating learning and overseeing individual development. The profile, role, status, and rewards of teachers differ significantly between the scenarios, and some imply a degree of change both towards and by teachers that may well prove uncomfortable to them and to society. One matter on which most would agree, however, is the imperative of avoiding the "meltdown" Scenario 6. How to devise new models of teacher professionalism and organisational roles, in ways that enhance the attractiveness of the job, the commitment of teachers, and the effectiveness of schools as learning organisations? How to attract new blood into the profession?

What is the best way for schools to lay the foundation for lifelong learning?

Schools and lifelong learning. The principle of integrating school policy and practice into the larger lifelong learning framework is now widely agreed, for the benefit both of schooling and of lifelong learning strategies. It is less clear what this means in practice and the extent of change it implies. The scenarios suggest contrasting possibilities such as shorter, more intensive school careers compared with an extended initial education; diversified agencies, professionals, and programmes compared with highly focused knowledge-based approaches. Behind these choices lie further questions. Does the task of laying firm foundations for lifelong learning call for fundamentally different approaches by schools? Or instead, is it tantamount to a restatement of a demanding equality objective – ensuring that the quality resources and opportunities presently enjoyed only by the best-served are available to *all* students? ■

References

BARBER, M. (2000), "The Evidence of Things not Seen: Reconceptualising Public Education", Keynote Address at the OECD/Netherlands Rotterdam International Conference on Schooling for Tomorrow, 1-3 November (see CERI website at www.oecd.org/cer).

CARNOY, M. (2001), "Work, Society, Family, and Learning for the Future", forthcoming in OECD, *Schooling for Tomorrow: Trends and Scenarios*, Paris.

CASTELLS, M. (1996), *The Rise of the Network Society. The Information Age: Economy, Society and Culture*, Vol. 1, Cambridge, MA.

EUROPEAN COMMISSION, EURYDICE, EUROSTAT (2000), *Key Data on Education in Europe*, Office for Official Publications of the European Communities, Brussels/Luxembourg.

HARGREAVES, D.H. (1999), "Schools and the Future: the Key Role of Innovation", *Innovating Schools*, OECD, Paris, Chapter 3.

HUTMACHER, W. (1999), "Invariants and Change in Schools and Education Systems", *Innovating Schools*, OECD, Paris, Chapter 2.

JOHANSSON, Y. (2000), "Chair's Conclusions", from the OECD/Netherlands Rotterdam International Conference on Schooling for Tomorrow, 1-3 November (see CERI website at www.oecd.org/cer).

KENNEDY, K. J. (2001), "A New Century and the Challenges it brings for Young People: How might Schools support Youth in the Future?", forthcoming in OECD, *Schooling for Tomorrow: Trends and Scenarios*, Paris.

MICHEL, A. (2001), "Schools for an Emerging New World", forthcoming in OECD, *Schooling for Tomorrow: Trends and Scenarios*, Paris.

OECD (1994), *The OECD Jobs Study, Evidence and Explanations, Part I: Labour Market Trends and Underlying Forces for Change*, Paris.

OECD (1999), "Technology in Education: Trends, investment, access and use", *Education Policy Analysis*, Chapter 3, Paris.

OECD (2000a), *Learning to Bridge the Digital Divide*, CERI, Paris.

OECD (2000b), *Knowledge Management in the Learning Society*, CERI, Paris.

OECD (2000c), *Education at a Glance – OECD Indicators*, CERI, Paris.

OECD (2000d), *Employment Outlook*, Paris.

OECD (2001a), *Schooling for Tomorrow: Trends and Scenarios*, forthcoming, CERI, Paris.

OECD (2001b), *The Well-being of Nations: the role of human and social capital*, CERI, Paris.

PUTNAM, R. (2000), *Bowling Alone: The Collapse and Revival of American Community*, Simon Schuster, New York.

Statistical Annex

DATA FOR THE FIGURES

Chapter 1

Data for Figure 1.1 **Participation in education and training over the life-span in OECD countries[1]**

Percentage of age cohort enrolled in formal education (age 3 to 29) and participation in adult education and training (age 16 to 65), unweighted mean for 18 countries, 1998

	Enrolment in formal education								Participation in adult education and training						
Age groups	3-5	6-7	8-12	13-15	16-18	19-21	22-24	25-29	30-34	35-39	40-44	45-49	50-54	55-59	60-65
Australia[2]	50.13	100.22	99.52	98.77	83.78	50.58	28.59	18.94							
					76.72	63.26	44.75	42.97	41.54	39.44	41.31	33.93	29.74	24.74	14.11
Belgium Flem. Com. Flanders[2]	98.02	96.69	96.01	95.84	89.23	55.21	22.33	7.79							
					0.00	18.31	26.26	25.87	24.63	22.39	22.08	23.09	22.65	16.49	9.17
Canada[3]	44.03	96.75	98.33	100.36	80.63	41.25	24.08	9.80							
					78.41	63.16	51.02	48.68	40.63	40.28	43.62	29.75	33.99	27.05	10.09
Czech Republic	71.91	100.00	100.00	99.95	81.83	26.91	17.27	5.77							
					32.19	25.49	30.01	31.60	33.58	27.71	30.84	33.22	26.82	17.09	5.14
Denmark	84.38	97.11	99.73	98.79	82.79	45.44	36.30	18.93							
					66.11	65.88	62.85	66.91	61.32	59.21	67.49	63.44	52.53	41.51	24.13
Finland	37.65	84.08	99.60	99.87	89.06	45.86	43.50	21.32							
					72.71	67.77	70.88	71.07	70.54	67.58	63.43	61.11	53.87	41.82	20.18
Germany[3]	77.40	96.10	99.15	99.57	91.80	50.61	29.08	12.26							
					8.03	23.85	22.51	20.28	23.35	22.72	21.18	19.87	15.66	14.00	3.69
Hungary	84.77	99.90	100.52	96.97	81.56	35.48	15.88	6.14							
					25.44	31.84	28.70	29.39	24.55	22.81	16.94	19.51	15.51	7.68	0.00
Ireland[3]	52.76	100.35	99.72	100.90	82.14	41.87	14.56	6.61							
					37.06	36.70	33.12	30.29	26.41	28.37	22.33	19.49	19.57	12.59	5.41
Netherlands[3]	65.98	99.31	99.28	99.37	88.46	57.66	28.99	9.36							
					41.22	42.19	57.09	49.41	43.34	42.84	38.65	34.64	29.19	18.00	16.38
New Zealand	93.19	101.66	99.02	96.60	72.13	42.44	21.51	12.17							
					79.40	66.55	61.48	55.26	50.29	51.71	49.70	44.42	45.96	36.21	18.53
Norway	73.25	99.42	99.20	99.56	92.03	49.26	35.94	15.31							
					58.35	69.35	54.06	55.54	54.63	52.99	55.53	50.45	45.34	33.07	18.83
Poland[3]	29.95	100.14	97.91	96.69	85.07	46.49	24.76	7.17							
					16.05	14.03	18.72	21.55	15.45	17.79	16.91	17.11	9.49	5.20	0.45
Portugal	61.58	108.04	111.79	104.18	78.34	41.98	23.29	9.60							
					22.22	15.55	24.88	28.37	22.30	13.56	10.17	9.72	10.58	4.19	5.07
Sweden[3]	66.44	95.88	101.02	99.13	97.10	42.20	36.80	22.49							
					54.31	43.58	45.87	56.06	55.30	59.49	62.88	57.07	58.82	48.01	25.43
Switzerland[4]	39.35	100.02	100.19	99.06	86.32	43.52	22.09	10.13							
					33.94	60.95	50.34	55.74	47.20	42.70	46.78	41.88	35.82	29.46	21.99
United Kingdom[2]	81.68	99.12	98.84	99.23	66.31	40.67	18.76	11.77							
					71.35	53.55	57.28	55.79	51.87	51.05	56.63	47.22	35.14	29.60	16.26
United States[3]	58.91	102.62	101.30	101.49	74.84	42.79	25.51	11.56							
					44.68	47.76	49.86	46.56	45.03	44.64	47.37	45.56	42.51	34.34	19.52
Country mean	**65.08**	**98.75**	**100.06**	**99.24**	**83.52**	**44.46**	**26.07**	**12.06**							
					45.45	**44.99**	**43.87**	**43.96**	**40.66**	**39.30**	**39.66**	**36.19**	**32.40**	**24.50**	**13.02**

1. The data combine two very different concepts and coverage, one based on full-time education and the other largely on part-time participation, defined as participation in any organised learning activity over a twelve-month period.

The formal education data are drawn from national records of students enrolled in educational institutions and refer to 1998. In countries where students may enrol in more than one programme or there are differences in the reference dates for the population and enrolment surveys, participation estimates may exceed 100 per cent.

The adult education and training data are based on responses to a question in the International Adult Literacy Survey (IALS) on participation in any organised learning activity for any length of time during the previous twelve months and refer to 1998 (or earlier in some countries). Full-time students aged 16-24 are excluded.

2. Adult education and training data, 1996.

3. Adult education and training data, 1994.

4. Adult education and training data, German- and French-speaking populations, 1994; Italian-speaking population, 1998.

Source: OECD Education Database and International Adult Literacy Survey Database.

Chapter 2

Data for Figure 2.1
Participation in pre-primary education[1] for children aged 3, 1998

	Net enrolment rate (%)
Australia	26.01
Austria	33.28
Belgium (Flem. Com.)	98.09
Czech Republic	43.60
Denmark	70.55
Finland	32.68
France	99.99
Germany	61.79
Hungary	68.25
Iceland	84.29
Ireland	2.82
Italy	95.21
Japan	57.27
Korea	7.66
Mexico	11.94
New Zealand	81.09
Norway	67.32
Poland	20.93
Portugal	52.27
Spain	71.62
Sweden	61.53
Switzerland	5.75
Turkey	0.43
United Kingdom	50.25
United States	35.79
Weighted average	38.20

1. The data refer to participation in organised centre-based instruction programmes primarily covering children aged 3 to compulsory school age. Programmes organised as day care, play groups and home-based structured and developmental activities are not included, and participation in programmes organised through health or social welfare ministries or privately are not, in all countries, reported.

Source: OECD (2000), *Education at a Glance - OECD Indicators*, Chart C1.2.

Data for Figure 2.3
Literacy scores[1] and under-achievement rates[2] of population aged 16-25 with upper secondary education, 1994-98

	Mean literacy score on document scale	Percentage of persons scoring at document literacy level 1 or 2
Australia	296.0	29.0
Belgium (Flanders)	304.8	19.8
Canada	305.3	25.7
Czech Republic	307.5	23.4
Denmark	320.4	10.3
Finland	324.6	9.9
Germany	309.7	19.7
Hungary	275.4	49.3
Ireland	281.8	41.8
Netherlands	312.4	13.4
New Zealand	288.1	37.1
Norway	307.2	23.2
Poland	270.8	51.7
Portugal	289.2	34.6
Sweden	314.1	21.4
Switzerland	299.4	31.2
United Kingdom	288.2	35.0
United States	274.2	58.6

1. Literacy scores are based on results for the document scale which tested the knowledge and skills required to locate and use information contained in various formats such as official forms, timetables, maps and charts. Scores are on a scale with a range of 0-500. The tests were administered in participating countries over the 1994-98 period.
2. Percentage performing below literacy level 3 (275 or below) on document scale.

Source: International Adult Literacy Survey Database; OECD and Statistics Canada (2000), *Literacy in the Information Age*, Table 3.5.

Data for Figures 2.2 and 2.4 Progress towards achieving a minimum educational attainment level and increasing tertiary qualifications, 1998

	Year	Percentage completing at least upper secondary education[1]				Percentage completing at least tertiary education[2]			
		25-64 year-olds	25-29 year-olds	50-54 year-olds	Ratio 25-29/50-54	25-64 year-olds	30-34 year-olds	50-54 year-olds	Ratio 30-34/50-54
Australia	1998	56	68	50	1.35	25	27	23	1.19
Austria	1997	73	84	68	1.24	11	13	10	1.41
Belgium	1998	57	77	48	1.61	25	32	21	1.54
Canada	1998	80	87	73	1.19	39	45	35	1.28
Czech Republic	1998	85	93	84	1.11	10	11	9	1.21
Denmark	1998	79	87	77	1.14	25	28	26	1.09
Finland	1997	68	85	58	1.47	29	36	26	1.41
France[3]	1998	61	78	53	1.47	21	26	17	1.53
Germany	1998	84	87	..	..	23	25	..	..
Greece	1997	44	70	32	2.19	16	23	11	2.02
Hungary	1998	63	78	61	1.28	13	14	15	0.94
Iceland	1998	55	56	48	1.16	21	29	14	2.08
Ireland	1998	51	70	37	1.88	21	27	15	1.79
Italy	1998	41	58	31	1.90	9	10	8	1.26
Japan	1998	80	..	..	..	30	..	..	..
Korea	1998	65	94	40	2.33	22	33	12	2.82
Mexico	1998	21	27	14	1.91	13	16	8	1.91
Netherlands	1998	64	75	58	1.31	24	26	23	1.15
New Zealand	1998	73	79	66	1.20	27	28	26	1.06
Norway	1997	83	92	76	1.21	26	29	23	1.23
Poland	1998	54	63	50	1.27	11	12	11	1.03
Portugal	1998	20	34	12	2.70	9	9	6	1.50
Spain	1998	33	57	19	2.97	20	28	12	2.34
Sweden	1998	76	88	71	1.24	28	30	27	1.14
Switzerland	1998	81	89	78	1.15	23	27	22	1.22
Turkey	1998	18	26	12	2.19	6	7	6	1.10
United Kingdom[3]	1998	60	64	55	1.16	24	25	21	1.22
United States	1998	86	88	86	1.03	35	36	36	1.02
Average		61	72	52	1.56	21	24	18	1.44

1. Excluding short programmes at upper secondary level.
2. Including tertiary-type A, tertiary-type B and advanced research programmes.
3. Includes some upper secondary programmes that do not meet classification requirements. See OECD (1999), *Classifying Educational Programmes, Manual for ISCED-97 Implementation in OECD Countries*.

Source: OECD Labour Force Survey Database (2000).

Data for Figure 2.5
Adult share in formal education by level, 1998

Percentage of adults aged 35 and over in enrolment

	All levels	Lower or upper secondary	Tertiary
Australia	12.02	16.80	20.98
Austria	1.47	0.00	9.79
Belgium (Flem. Com.)	4.77	11.21	3.01
Canada	3.46	2.02	11.99
Denmark	2.75	2.52	11.95
Finland	4.39	3.26	15.27
Germany	1.03	0.00	8.28
Iceland	2.92	3.68	15.00
Italy	0.65	0.08	3.54
Japan	0.43	0.21	2.17
Korea	0.66	0.00	2.87
Luxembourg	0.00	0.04	0.00
Mexico	0.54	1.22	2.78
Netherlands	2.34	3.45	7.31
New Zealand	6.04	5.24	23.86
Norway	3.11	1.57	15.06
Portugal	1.91	0.92	7.60
Spain	1.18	0.62	5.02
Sweden	7.97	11.70	18.98
Switzerland	0.55	0.00	5.06
Turkey	0.65	0.00	5.93
United Kingdom	8.49	11.93	22.21
United States	4.08	0.69	16.43

Source: OECD Education database.

Data for Figure 2.6
Adult participation in continuing education and training, 1994-98

	Participation rate[1]	Average hours of training per participant
Australia	38.8	264
Belgium (Flanders)	21.2	129
Canada	37.7	305
Czech Republic	25.5	168
Denmark	55.7	220
Finland	56.8	213
Hungary	19.3	188
Ireland	24.3	332
Netherlands	37.4	242
New Zealand	47.5	284
Norway	47.9	240
Poland	13.9	149
Portugal	14.2	m
Sweden	52.5	m
Switzerland	41.8	140
United Kingdom	43.9	214
United States	39.7	170

1. Full-time students aged 16-24 and people who obtained less than 6 hours of training are excluded.
Source: OECD and Statistics Canada (2000), *Literacy in the Information Age*, Table 3.11.

Data for Figure 2.7
Learning by older adults after formal education, 1994-98

Percentage of 46 to 65 year-olds with only upper secondary education performing at literacy level 3 or above (document scale)[1]

	Percentage of persons who scored below 325 on document literacy scale	Percentage of persons who scored above or equal to 325 on document literacy scale
Australia	90.8	9.2
Belgium (Flanders)	87.5	12.5
Canada	86.6	13.4
Czech Republic	79.2	20.8
Denmark	89.9	10.1
Finland	86.2	13.9
Germany	89.7	10.3
Hungary	96.3	3.7
Ireland	88.0	12.0
Netherlands	83.3	16.8
New Zealand	76.9	23.1
Norway	86.3	13.7
Poland	96.8	3.2
Portugal	94.4	5.6
Sweden	76.7	23.3
Switzerland	92.7	7.3
United Kingdom	76.4	23.6
United States	90.6	9.4

1. Literacy scores are based on results for the document scale which tested the knowledge and skills required to locate and use information contained in various formats such as official forms, timetables, maps and charts. Scores are on a scale with a range of 0-500. The tests were administered in participating countries over the 1994-98 period.
Source: International Adult Literacy Survey Database.

Data for Figure 2.8
Trends in expenditure per student and enrolment in primary, secondary and tertiary education, 1990-96

(1990=100)	Primary and secondary education		Tertiary education	
	Expenditure per student	Enrolment	Expenditure per student	Enrolment
Australia	114	104	114	129
Austria[1]	120	105	109	118
Canada	104	108	93	121
Czech Republic	m	134	m	150
Finland	86	104	98	130
France	113	99	100	129
Ireland	136	97	107	156
Italy	95	89	70	126
Korea	m	89	m	139
Mexico	166	104	101	122
Netherlands	110	98	89	113
New Zealand	m	108	m	150
Norway	114	97	94	148
Portugal	153	89	56	268
Spain[1]	125	91	127	115
Switzerland[1]	101	106	86	116
United Kingdom	101	109	84	176

m: data not available.
All data are classified according to ISCED-76. See OECD (1999), *Classifying Educational Programmes, Manual for ISCED-97 Implementation in OECD Countries.*
1. Public institutions only.
Source: OECD (2000), *Education at a Glance - OECD Indicators*, Table B4.3.

Data for Figures 2.9a and 2.9b
Trends in public and private expenditure on all levels of education and on tertiary education, 1990-96

Index of change in expenditure (1990=100)

	All levels of education		Tertiary education	
	Direct public expenditure for educational institutions	Direct private expenditure for educational institutions	Direct public expenditure for educational institutions	Direct private expenditure for educational institutions
Australia	120	168	132	190
Austria	129	m	128	m
Belgium (Flem. Com.)	112	m	109	m
Canada	108	141	98	145
Denmark	124	235	113	x
Finland	97	x	128	x
France	117	105	132	115
Hungary	61	122	56	235
Ireland	139	139	164	167
Italy	82	m	74	m
Mexico	137	m	92	m
Netherlands	106	118	97	126
New Zealand	123	m	107	m
Norway	115	m	132	m
Portugal	147	m	147	m
Spain	119	154	140	201
Switzerland	106	m	99	m
United Kingdom	113	m	114	752

m: Data not available.
x: Data included in another category.

Source: OECD (2000), Education at a Glance – OECD Indicators, Table B1.2.

Table 2.A
Labour market training: public expenditure and participant inflows[1]

	Expenditure as a percentage of GDP	Participant Inflows as a percentage of the labour force
Australia (1997-98)	0.05	1.9 (0.2)
Austria (1999)	0.19 (0.02)	3.0
Belgium (1998)	0.26 (0.09)	8.7 (6.1)
Canada (1997-98)	0.15	1.6
Czech Republic (1999)	0.01	0.4
Denmark (1999)	0.98 (0.21)	19.8 (8.1)
Finland (1999)	0.38 (0.04)	4.0
France (1998)	0.31 (0.03)	2.8 (0.6)
Germany (1999)	0.35	1.3
Greece (1997)	0.06	m
Hungary (1999)	0.07	1.4 (0.1)
Ireland (1996)	0.21 (0.08)	4.1 (2.5)
Italy (1999)	0.25	m
Japan (1998-99)	0.03	m
Korea (1998)	0.10 (0.02)	4.6 (1.9)
Luxembourg (1997)	0.01	0.6 (0.1)
Mexico (1999)	0.04 (0.01)	3.4 (2.0)
Netherlands (1998)	0.31 (0.03)	3.3 (0.9)
New Zealand (1998-99)	0.24	3.3
Norway (1999)	0.05	1.0
Poland (1998)	0.02	0.8
Portugal (1998)	0.30 (0.22)	9.9 (9.3)
Spain (1999)	0.22 (0.10)	11.3 (9.6)
Sweden (1999)	0.49 (0.01)	3.9 (0.6)
Switzerland (1998)	0.19	m
United Kingdom (1997-98)	0.07 (0.01)	0.9
United States (1998-99)	0.04	0.6

m: data not available.
1. Figures in parentheses are for employed workers.
Source: OECD (2000), Employment Outlook, Table H.

Table 2.B
Adult participation in continuing education and training

	Total participation rate[1] (adults aged 16-65)
Finland	56.8
Denmark	55.7
Sweden	52.5
Norway	47.9
New Zealand	47.5
United Kingdom	43.9
Switzerland	41.8
United States	39.7
Australia	38.8
Canada	37.7
Netherlands	37.4
Czech Republic	25.5
Ireland	24.3
Belgium (Flanders)	21.2
Hungary	19.3
Portugal	14.2
Poland	13.9

1. Full-time students aged 16-24 and people who obtained less than 6 hours of training are excluded.
Source: OECD and Statistics Canada (2000), Literacy in the Information Age, Table 3.11.

Table 2.C
Shifts in public support at the tertiary level for institutions and learners between 1990 and 1996

	Direct expenditure for all types of institutions	Scholarships and other grants to students/households	Student loans
Australia	133	189	140
Austria	130	169	a
Belgium (Flem. Com.)	109	m	a
Canada	100	185	282
Denmark	115	123	106
Finland	130	193	n
France	134	167	a
Hungary	66	114	a
Iceland	113	m	23
Ireland	166	127	n
Italy	76	m	m
Mexico	110	119	m
Netherlands	99	75	139
Norway	135	153	119
New Zealand	108	82	m
Poland	71	m	m
Portugal	149	m	m
Spain	143	174	n
Sweden	184	179	169
Switzerland	99	95	78
United Kingdom	117	200	m

m: data not available;
n: magnitude is either negligible or zero.
a: data not applicable because the category does not apply.
Source: OECD Education Database.

Chapter 3

Data for Figure 3.1
College entrance by family income, United States, 1972-96

Percentage of high-school completers aged 16-24 who were enrolled in college the October after completing high school

	Low	Middle	High
1972	26.1	42.5	63.8
1973	20.3	40.9	64.4
1975	31.2	46.2	64.5
1977	27.7	44.2	66.3
1979	30.5	43.2	63.2
1981	33.6	49.2	67.6
1983	34.6	45.2	70.3
1985	40.2	50.6	74.6
1987	36.9	50.0	73.8
1989	48.1	55.4	70.7
1990	46.7	54.4	76.6
1991	39.5	58.4	78.2
1992	40.9	57.0	79.0
1993	50.4	56.9	79.3
1994	41.0	57.8	78.4
1995	34.2	56.1	83.4
1996	48.6	62.7	78.0

Source: NCES – National Centre for Education Statistics (2000), "Quick Tables and Figures".

Data for Figure 3.2
The relative earnings of women in successive generations

Mean annual earnings of women as a percentage of men's earnings at the same educational level, ages 30-44 and 55-64, 1998

		Least educated Below upper secondary		Most educated University-type programme	
		Ages 30-44	Ages 55-64	Ages 30-44	Ages 55-64
Australia	1997	60	55	66	57
Canada	1997	52	53	70	58
Czech Republic	1998	66	58	67	63
Denmark	1997	74	72	75	73
Finland	1996	77	80	71	70
France	1998	68	65	71	65
Germany	1997	60	52	69	59
Hungary	1998	77	81	61	74
Ireland	1997	64	67	94	90
Italy	1995	69	72	57	37
Netherlands	1996	47	42	61	48
New Zealand	1998	53	44	66	41
Norway	1997	64	66	61	64
Portugal	1997	73	71	76	70
Spain	1995	62	m	73	m
Sweden	1997	72	72	65	66
Switzerland	1998	54	44	63	51
United Kingdom	1998	45	45	62	62
United States	1998	53	52	62	44

Source: OECD (2000), Education at a Glance – OECD Indicators, Table E5.2.

Data for Figure 3.3
College entrance by racial or ethnic group, United States, 1972-96

Percentage of high-school completers aged 16-24 who were enrolled in college the October after completing high school

	White	Black	Hispanic
1972	49.7	44.6	45.0
1973	47.8	32.5	54.1
1975	51.1	41.7	58.0
1977	50.8	49.5	50.8
1979	49.9	46.7	45.0
1981	54.9	42.7	52.1
1983	55.0	38.2	54.2
1985	60.1	42.2	51.0
1987	58.6	52.2	33.5
1989	60.7	53.4	55.1
1990	63.0	46.8	42.7
1991	65.4	46.4	57.2
1992	64.3	48.2	55.0
1993	62.9	55.6	62.2
1994	64.5	50.8	49.1
1995	64.3	51.2	53.7
1996	67.4	56.0	50.8

Source : NCES – National Center for Education Statistics (2000), "Quick Tables and Figures".

Data for Figure 3.4
Home and school access to computers in OECD countries, 1998

	Percentage of households possessing a PC	Students per computer in upper secondary education
Australia[1]	48	
Belgium	35	
Belgium (Flem. Com.)[a]		13
Belgium (Fr. Com.)[b]*		26
Canada[b]*	45	6
Czech Republic[b]		10
Denmark[2,a]	63	9
Finland[1,a]	42	7
France[1,b]	23	7
Germany[1]	45	
Hungary[1]	26	
Iceland[b]	61	11
Ireland[a]		8
Italy[a]	20	14
Japan[b]		12
Korea[a]		24
Luxembourg[b]		12
Netherlands[a]	55	16
New Zealand	33	
Norway[b]		4
Portugal[a]		35
Spain	24	
United Kingdom[a]	33	9
United States[2,c]	51	6
Unweighted average	40	13

Data on percentage of households possessing a PC: 1. 1999. 2. 2000. Source: National statistic resources.	Data on students per computer in upper secondary education: *Country did not satisfy all sampling criteria. Sources (See References at the end of Chapter 3): a. OECD (1999d); b. IEA/SITES (1999); c. NCES (2000).

Data for Figure 3.5
Percentage of U.S. households with Internet access by racial and ethnic group, 1998 and 2000

	1998	2000
White	29.8	46.1
Black	11.2	23.5
Asian Americans & Pacific Islanders	36.0	56.8
Hispanic	12.6	23.6

Sources: NTIA (1999), Falling through the Net: Defining the Digital Divide.

Data for Figure 3.6
Home access to the Internet by gross income decile group in the UK, 1998-1999 and 1999-2000

	1998-1999	1999-2000
Lowest 10%	3	6
Second decile group	1	3
Third decile group	2	4
Fourth decile group	3	6
Fifth decile group	4	15
Sixth decile group	7	15
Seventh decile group	10	22
Eigth decile group	16	28
Ninth decile group	19	38
Highest 10%	32	48

Source: National Statistics, United Kingdom (2000), Internet Access.

Data for Figure 3.7 **Participation in job-related education and training by employed adults with different educational levels, 1994-95**

	Percentage participating		Average hours per trainee	
	Below upper secondary education	University education	Below upper secondary education	University education
Australia	30	60	102	122
Belgium (Flanders)	8	41		114
Canada	21	56	68	105
Ireland	16	41	214	135
Netherlands	24	49	129	127
New Zealand	41	69	137	132
Poland	9	33	103	141
Switzerland (Fr. Com.)	7	37		187
Switzerland (Ger. Com.)	11	45		93
United Kingdom	44	79	80	99
United States	19	70	92	83

Source: OECD (2000), Education of a Glance – OECD Indicators, Table C7.4.

Chapter 4

Data for Figure 4.1 **Increasing importance of knowledge-based industries, 1985 and 1997**

	Share in business sector value added		Share in business sector employment	
	1985	1997	1985	1997
Australia	41.9	46.2	39.2	43.4
Austria	38.7	42.3	25.6	29.5
Canada	44.3	48.8	33.7	38.2
Denmark	42.2	39.7	32.7	36.1
Finland	33.7	41.6	24.0	30.5
France	44.8	49.2	33.9	39.0
West Germany	50.8	57.9	37.6	42.5
Iceland	m	m	19.6	25.2
Italy	37.7	40.4	25.2	29.4
Mexico	35.3	37.9	28.7	28.9
Netherlands	46.7	47.4	40.2	42.5
New Zealand	m	m	43.6	49.6
Norway	m	m	29.7	32.2
Portugal	m	m	14.6	20.6
Spain	35.9	37.1	20.2	23.8
Sweden	45.2	48.1	33.6	37.1
United Kingdom	45.2	51.0	m	m
United States	51.9	52.3	43.1	47.5

m: data not available.
Source: OECD (2000), *Science, Technology and Industry Outlook*.

Data for Figure 4.2
Growth in the proportion of the population and employment with tertiary-level qualifications, 1989-96

Percentage point change in the share of individuals with tertiary education

		Working-age population	Employed workers
Australia	1989	2.80	3.58
Austria	1989	1.76	1.58
Belgium	1989	7.07	7.36
Canada	1989	6.90	6.77
Denmark	1989	4.22	3.89
Finland	1989	3.56	5.72
France	1989	5.38	6.09
Germany	1992	0.38	2.30
Ireland	1989	7.79	7.74
Italy	1990	2.46	3.39
Netherlands	1990	3.35	2.99
New Zealand	1989	2.43	0.56
Norway	1989	4.00	3.52
Portugal	1989	4.44	6.92
Spain	1989	8.21	10.78
Sweden	1989	4.09	5.69
Switzerland	1991	1.63	1.91
United Kingdom	1989	6.40	7.47
United States	1989	4.14	3.91

Source: OECD (2000), *Economic Outlook*.

Data for Figure 4.3
Upskilling in total employment growth, 1980-98

Average annual percentage change in total employment

	White-collar, high-skilled workers	Other workers	Total
Australia (1980-97)	0.49	1.23	1.72
Austria (1984-98)	0.15	0.85	1.01
Belgium (1983-97)	0.26	0.53	0.79
Canada (1980-98)	0.53	0.77	1.30
Finland (1980-98)	0.72	-0.74	-0.02
France (1982-95)	0.55	-0.51	0.04
Germany (1980-90)	0.55	-0.12	0.44
Greece (1981-97)	0.59	-0.10	0.48
Iceland (1991-98)	0.77	0.34	1.11
Ireland (1987-95)	0.80	0.92	1.72
Italy (1981-95)	0.28	-0.58	-0.30
Japan (1980-98)	0.72	0.19	0.91
Netherlands (1981-98)	1.32	0.80	2.11
New Zealand (1987-98)	0.26	0.67	0.93
Norway (1980-95)	0.73	-0.16	0.57
Portugal (1980-98)	0.42	0.58	0.99
Spain (1980-98)	0.76	-0.02	0.74
Sweden (1980-98)	0.52	-0.94	-0.41
Switzerland (1991-98)	1.08	-1.32	-0.24
United Kingdom (1991-98)	0.69	-0.32	0.37
United States (1980-98)	0.78	0.79	1.57

Sources: International Labour Office database (2000) and OECD (1998), *Technology, Productivity and Job Creation: Best Policy Practices*.

Data for Figure 4.4
Skill requirements of knowledge workers in five domains[1], Canada

	Mean	Standard error
Cognitive	1.83	0.56
Management	1.48	0.52
Communication	0.92	0.45
Gross physical	0.03	0.26
Fine physical	0.46	0.79

1. The scoring is based on the Canadian Classification and Dictionary of Occupations (CCDO) which give scores to 6 500 occupations according to the requirements of the job. There are 43 indices representing general education, physical abilities and other different aptitudes. Running a Principal Component Analysis gives a clustering of the indices and each cluster represents a specific skill. The best model gives the five skill domains.

The mean score is the difference between the average score of knowledge workers and the average score of all workers. For instance, the average score of cognitive skills of knowledge workers is 1.83 higher than the average score of cognitive skills required of all workers.

Source: Béjaoui (2000), *Sur la mesure des qualifications: application à l'émergence de l'économie du savoir*.

Also available

Early Childhood Education and Care (provisional title, forthcoming May 2001)

Education at a Glance – OECD Indicators 2001 (June 2001)

Education at a Glance – OECD Indicators 2000 (May 2000)

Education Policy Analysis 1999 (1999)

From Initial Education to Working Life – Making Transitions Work (2000)

Investing in Competencies for All: Analysis of the 1999 World Education Indicators (2000)

Learning to Bridge the Digital Divide (2000)

Knowledge Management in the Learning Society (2000)

Literacy, Economy and Society: First Results from the International Adult Literacy Survey (1995)

Literacy for the Knowledge Economy: Further Results from the International Adult Literacy Survey (1997)

Literacy in the Information Age: Final Report of the International Adult Literacy Survey (2000)

Measuring Student Knowledge and Skills: A New Framework for Assessment (1999)

Measuring Student Knowledge and Skills: The PISA 2000 Assessment of Reading, Mathematical and Scientific Literacy (2000)

Motivating Students for Lifelong Learning (2000)

Overcoming Exclusion through Adult Learning (1999)

Schooling for Tomorrow: Trends and Scenarios (forthcoming May 2001)

Special Needs Education Statistics (2000)

The Well-being of Nations: the Role of Human and Social Capital (May 2001)

Where are the Resources for Lifelong Learning? (2000)

OECD PUBLICATIONS, 2, rue André-Pascal, 75775 PARIS CEDEX 16
PRINTED IN FRANCE
(96 2001 03 1 P) ISBN 92-64-09-18636-0 – No. 51709 2001